Preschool Confidential

Also by Sandi Kahn Shelton

Sleeping Through the Night . . . And Other Lies
You Might As Well Laugh

Preschool Confidential

Sandi Kahn Shelton

St. Martin's Press
New York

www.stmartins.com

Design by Heidi Eriksen

Library of Congress Cataloging-in-Publication Data

Shelton, Sandi Kahn.
    Preschool confidential / Sandi Kahn Shelton. — 1st ed.
      p. cm.
    ISBN 0-312-25458-X
    1. Toddlers. 2. Preschool children. 3. Parenting—Humor. 4. Parent and child—Humor. I. Title

HQ774.5.S54 2001
649'.123—dc21   2001019156

First Edition: May 2001

10 9 8 7 6 5 4 3 2 1

To Jimbo,
whose love and laughter sustain me always

Contents

Contents

Contents

Acknowledgments

Thinking about preschoolers has given me great pleasure for the last few months, and I owe a debt of gratitude to many people, especially those who were patiently waiting for dinner while I was still writing. My own three children, Benjamin, Allison, and Stephanie, have kept me hugely entertained through the years with the hilarious things they say and do, and have also been loving and patient and amused as I told the stories of their childhoods.

Special thanks go to Regula Noetzli and Jennifer Enderlin, my agent and editor, respectively, who are unfailingly encouraging as well as fun to talk to on the phone.

I am very grateful to all of those who have shared their preschoolers' stories with me over the years, and who have listened to mine: Alice Mattison, Kay Kudlinski, Gwen Myers, Tracy Blanford, Sandy and Bryan Connolly, Kate Flanagan, Mary Rose Meade, Nancy Hall, Leslie Connor, Alix Boyle, Andrea Atkins Hessekiel, Sherry and Jack Ellis, Laurie Hutchinson, Karen Vlock, Maria Amendola, Jane Tamarkin, Linda Shelton, Nadine Shimada, Jill Bergquist, Barb Pavelko, Kathy Parker, Cathy Scherer, Karen Bergantino, Melissa Balmain, Sari Bode, Alice Elliott Smith, Mary Barton Sigworth, Sue Amarante, Kim Caldwell Steffen, Jack Hitt, Andrea Higgins, Suzanne Reddick, Beth Lyons, and Jet Rogers. My own three moms, Joan Graham, Helen Myers, and Pat Shelton, have contributed lots of funny stories of survival. And many other friends have given advice, oases of sanity, and emotional support, and I couldn't have completed this book without them: Diane Cyr, Mary Squibb, Jennifer Smith, Caroline Rosenstone, Deborah Hare, Bobbi Harshav, Tammy Lytle, Ida Massenburg, Rick Sandella, Fran Fried, Laura Collins-Hughes, and Carolyn Wyman.

Introduction

Welcome to being the parent of a preschool child. I know you're tired, but think of this: At least you've survived teething, colic, and walking around in public with spit-up on all your clothing. By now, you have changed 49 million stinky diapers (20 million of those in public) and have learned to get your required sleep in ten-second intervals between wails.

And now your kid is three and verbal and also fairly certain she's ready to get her own apartment, now that she no longer looks like Dwight Eisenhower. She just has a few questions for you before she signs the lease.

"Why do people have red cars? Mommy! Are red cars working cars? Do cows think about red cars? Sometimes? Why is that man crossing the street? Why don't we have all the cars in the world at our house? Why, Mommy? Why is that boy walking? What are all the fishes doing right now? What about mans who fix roofs? Do mans who fix roofs know their phone number? Why? Do bad guys get lots of ice cream? Can we kill bad guys if we want to? Why, Mommy? Will bad guys kill us? How many bugs are there? If our roof breaks, will we know the man's phone number?"

Naturally you don't have the answers to any of these questions. Even if you're relatively certain you could find a roofer's telephone number if you needed one, by the time that one semirational question gets asked, you are so baffled by the stream of consciousness of the earlier questions that you are quite speechless and looking for a place to curl up and take a nap.

Someone—probably now in a padded cell somewhere—once documented the fact that preschoolers ask 437 questions a day. We can't know how this research was accomplished, but somehow I can't get the image out of my head of a beleaguered scientist, bug-eyed and holding a clicker and tallying up the questions until he dropped to the floor in a coma. Sometimes science requires the ultimate sacrifice.

Anyway, it should be noted that 437 per day was simply the *average* number of questions. Many children—probably yours included—ask this many before breakfast. By the time they have a good head of steam going—say, around 11:00 A.M., they can easily crank the total up to over a thousand on a good day. As to the fate of the researchers, I think the chances are good that they are probably living on a desert island somewhere, hoping that no one finds them and asks them anything ever again.

But don't worry. You might think that 437 questions is too many for you personally to handle; you may think that after Question #300, for instance, you might start checking the want ads to see if the merchant marines are hiring these days. But you only rarely see parents going off on overseas assignments. Nature mercifully arranges it that after Question #246, your brain goes numb and you hardly even mind after that. In fact, you'll discover that there are stock answers that seem to work for most questions. Even with your eyes glazed over, you can deliver the old standbys:

- "I don't think so."
- "My, that *would* be amazing!"

- "No one really knows."
- "We can't because we're civilized humans."
- "Because I said so, and I'm bigger than you are."

Once you master rotating these simple phrases, believe me, you can turn off your brain and try to regain some sense of who it was you used to be before you had children. I know, I know. It's incredible that just five simple phrases can totally take care of all your conversational needs, but it's true. Just be sure that you don't start agreeing to things without really grasping what's been said to you. Once my friend Paul found he'd agreed to turn on the washing machine with the hamster inside.

That's what having a little child is like. You find yourself uttering phrases that you can't believe you would ever say—things like, "If you don't stop jumping on the kitchen counter with Barbie's leg in your hand, you're going to put out your eye and then I won't take you to the circus."

Besides learning some stock phrases, there are other skills you're going to acquire, too, things you didn't ever think you'd need to learn but now find indispensable to getting along in the world. Getting a kid out of a toy store, for instance, is of paramount importance, and you'd like it if the legal authorities didn't get called in to observe just how you do this. You learn after a while to master the Surprise Exit—suddenly whirling around and picking up your child and, while talking nonstop in a bright, almost pharmaceutically enhanced voice, charging out of the toy store full speed ahead with the kid in a football hold under your arm. If you're lucky, it won't be until you're halfway home that the kid catches his breath and realizes he's been swindled out of a perfectly good screaming opportunity.

Oh, you're going to get good at a lot of new things: Glaring While Smiling, which is the art of warning your child of some dire consequence while appearing to the public to be having a perfectly lovely conversation. And saying, "Do. Not. Do. That. Again," in the precise tone of voice that your mother used. You might even find a use for that old chestnut: "Stop crying, or I'll give you something to cry about!"—a statement that means absolutely nothing but is pleasantly ominous just the same.

Just remember this while your ears are ringing with questions: three-year-olds are the pinnacle of human adorability. That alone probably accounts for the fact that more of them aren't shipped off to Grandma's house with no return address.

They know this about themselves, too, deep down in that I'm-little-and-the-world-is-my-oyster way they have. They see clearly that you have always in love with them, and they sense that, without sacrificing any cuteness whatsoever, they have amassed even more power—now that they have acquired human speech as well as the physical skills to dismantle your car engine, a triple-A battery, and your microwave oven in one afternoon.

The bad news is that your child is no longer just a cute little accessory that you can carry along in a padded carrier, while *you* look both debonair and domesticated. You're now readily identifiable as a Parent—and chances are, you've scared quite a few childless people into being even more conscientious about their birth control. You know things you never thought you'd know: how to get a ham sandwich out of the VCR, how many Arthur Glow-in-the-Dark Band-Aids can fit on one child boo-boo, and what lies you need to tell simply to get a baby-sitter to agree to come to your house.

But here's the good news: preschoolers are hilarious— and if you can somehow not mind the fact that they're putting the kitty in the dryer and squirting shaving cream all over the bathroom, you'll have a lot of good laughs ahead of you.

And here's what else: Nobody's cuter when sleeping than a little child. Sometimes that's good enough to get you through another day.

1

And Baby Turns Three

It talks!

I adore three-year-olds. I adore them even though it's obvious that they are power-packed little automaton terrorists sent to ransack our world and toy with our sanity. We know this about them through years of documenting their activities. Still, I say you have to be willing to overlook some things in life.

At least by the time they're three, even though you know they're determined to make you crazy, you can have conversations with them instead of having them screech at you from some vague, incomprehensible, and unhappy world. For instance, now when they imagine it would be terrific to have their oatmeal rubbed into their hair—and who wouldn't want that?—they can discuss it with you, rather than just arching their backs and flailing around trying to get the bowl to land precisely on their heads and holding *you* responsible when that doesn't work.

It's so much more pleasant to have someone say to you, "Mother, now I believe I would like to have some cooked oats smeared throughout my hair but not quite running into my eyes, if you could please manage that," rather than simply slipping into a full-blown rage and flinging a bowl at your own personal head. And even if her verbal skills aren't what you would desire, still—"Food on head *now*" communicates all you need to know.

Sometimes, of course, conversations with three-year-olds veer off into a bizarre world that you'd rather not visit—sort of like chatting with someone who's a cross between Salvador Dalí, the Unabomber, and Baby Bop, all of whom have had too much to drink. But by and large, three years old marks the beginning of a new era. You catch your first glimpse of the fact that you are raising an actual human being, one that will someday go off into the world and understand the international banking system, for all you know. This—this *baby* is someday going to turn into a regular citizen. You stop holding your breath about the Crib Death thing and the Swallowing Small Objects thing and the Tipping Over in the Car Seat thing and a lot of other worries that have made you wake up in the middle of the night with your eyeballs bulging out of your head.

Never mind that other worries replace those particular ones. College is inching ever closer, of course, and the cost is going up a bajillion dollars per year, besides which there's still eighth grade to get through and what if he wants to play the tuba or turns out to be the kind of guy that women despise and think it's something you did to him during the weaning process? And what if it *is* something you did?

But forget about all that. In the meantime, here's what you do know: You've created an actual small person, using only handy stuff you found around the house—and by God, it walks and talks and interacts and asks a zillion questions. Sometimes you're in slack-jawed awe at the marvel of such an accomplishment, and other times you're so tired you can't remember exactly what you did that caused this little person to get started in the first place.

And it's beginning to dawn on you that you're *always* going to be this tired, that that whole postpartum phase they told you would last six weeks is maybe a permanent condition. It's conceivable that those bags that have formed under your eyes are there to stay, and that, by some mysterious biochemical transfer, some very valuable real estate in your brain was eroded during the childbirth process.

Don't worry too much. As my friend Patricia once said, "All of this is going to pass. If they can be three, then they can be five. And if they can be five, then they can be eight. And if they can be eight, they can turn into teenagers. And teenagers are practically grown up."

I don't know what this means exactly, but it seemed to bring Patricia a measure of reassurance, and so I told her it made me feel better, too.

And it eats—some things, at least

Some three-year-olds have figured out that one of the essential ways to stay alive is to eat the food that Mommy and Daddy give them, as long as these foods are not green and are not overloaded with nutritional substances, such as vitamins and minerals. Usually small children specialize in macaroni and cheese and peanut butter, although some adventurous ones have been known to eat raisins—but only if they're allowed first to dissect the raisins and wear them for a while on the tips of their fingers.

Many three-year-olds, though, are still on the Toddler Diet Plan, which has much more variety and isn't as unimaginative as the regular human diet. On this menu plan, foods are to be enjoyed as a whole-body experience—rubbed into hair and skin, or stuffed underneath shirts (for those times when the route to the stomach through the esophagus seems so tedious).

A typical breakfast on the Toddler Diet Plan would consist of a bowl of corn flakes and milk—left to sit for half an hour so that each corn flake is holding the maximum amount of milk. (This is much like the concept of wine being left out to "breathe" and is absolutely essential.) Then three bites are taken and the rest is poured slowly and systematically onto the floor, where the dog licks it up. Afterward, for additional nutritional value, one must kiss the dog on the mouth, licking off any flakes that might have stuck to fur.

Lunch on the Toddler Diet Plan should consist of two bites of a banana (then the rest must be smashed and rubbed on shirt), a stick from the backyard (preferably moistened in a glass of Kool-Aid), and, if there's still room, a few bites of dog kibble. (The chicken flavor is recommended.) If a tomato is available, one may eat four of the seeds before yelling, "Yuck!" and rubbing the rest in hair. A typical afternoon snack would include a couple of crayons (orange and red are always top choices, but wrappers should be off) and a glass of milk (two sips and then the rest spilled on the shirt so it can be sucked later). Also, it's helpful to lick ten potato chips before storing them in the couch cushions for another day.

Dinner should be a stick of broccoli mashed up in apple juice, as well as any crumbs found under the kitchen table. A conscientious toddler will eat the breading off one chicken nugget, and throw the rest on the floor. If still hungry, one can always dredge up a cookie that was put in the toy box and which would be delicious if it were dipped in bathwater. And, of course, a few squirts of liquid soap always makes a nice garnish for a cookie.

For maximum culinary enjoyment, the evening can be polished off with a nightcap of toothpaste, at least one-quarter tube, washed down with tap water.

The two kinds of three-year-olds

Besides the fact that three-year-olds now feed themselves, the next best thing about having one of them is that people will stop telling you about the Terrible Twos. They will tell you instead that you're home free, that the worst is behind you. All the popular wisdom these days tells us that, compared to two-year-olds, people of three are sterling individuals of great character and dignity, and that they would no more drop to the floor in a tantrum and call for the imminent destruction of all mankind than—well, than *you* would.

It is wonderful to call an end to these Terrible Two discussions with strangers in the grocery store—but if you are thinking that your days of nuclear meltdowns in the vegetable aisle are over, then I'm afraid I may have just a little bad news for you.

Sometimes children *don't* go through the Terrible Twos. There are children who, for whatever reason, decide to skip that whole stage, and who stay marvelously reasonable throughout the time other kids are channeling Attila the Hun. Instead, they are submitting placidly to whatever suggestions you might make about their lives—even if it's something radical like not cutting their toast into precise triangles. These are children who don't even become unduly alarmed when they see you eat the last bite of the last apple in the house, or when they're looking for their teddy bear and you say, "Oh, darling, I put it in the washing machine today and it fell completely apart. So sorry!"

I've heard parents of these kinds of two-year-olds question the entire social system that insists on giving children such negative labels. They think calling a child's age "terrible" is a grievous wrong that should be righted by an act of Congress or something. My friend Leslie once told me, with tears in her eyes, that whole generations of two-year-old children have been maligned by parents' unfortunate expectations, all due to people's ignorant insistence on perpetuating such myths.

Then Leslie's daughter turned three. I was invited to the birthday party, and sighed in rapture along with all the other guests as little Chloe floated downstairs in a beautiful pink organdy dress with little lace-cuffed socks. There was, in retrospect, just the merest hint of a shadow falling across her face as she took one look at her pink frosted cake with "Chloe" written in purple script. But none of us expected what was coming next. In a voice like a drill sergeant, she screamed, "My cake! NO ONE will have any cake but ME! It's MY cake and MY day! Give me all the presents and GO HOME!"

Leslie gave me a panicked look. "This was just one isolated incident, right?" she said later. Her eyes were pleading. "This isn't the way it's going to be from now on! Tell me there's not something called the Terrible Threes."

"Of course not," I said. I'm afraid I do know of a few bad cases where a kid's true personality woke up at three, and for quite some time after that he was known as a holy terror. One friend of mine said her child was wonderful up until age three, and then began the stage she called The Terrible Rest of Her Life. But we must keep things in perspective: one incident can be simply an isolated event. Even, say, one hundred incidents can be just a phase. All you know for sure at the moment of the tantrum is that you're being visited once again by the current incarnation of Attila the Hun, and that he's ready to ransack. How long he's planning to stick around drinking bad whiskey and plundering is anybody's guess.

Toilet training ... at last ... finally, sort of

It used to be that if you didn't have a kid toilet trained by the age of one, then you were seen as kind of a derelict parent or, worse, as someone who believed it was okay for the human race to wet its pants. Apparently in other parenting eras, children were to be trotted off to potty chairs straight from the delivery room. Today, of course, no one believes that kind of thing—although there are still some people who will growl at you if, say, elementary school is looming and you haven't yet bought any training pants for the kid. After things were still seeming iffy when her son was five, one friend of mine decided that he would have to select a college based on their Remedial Toilet-Training program, something that's often not mentioned in the catalogs.

In reality, though, three-year-olds mostly have some notion of the potty, as well as an opinion as to whether they ever intend to make use of one or not. Many kids who couldn't be bothered at age two find, now that they are world citizens of Three Years Old, that they would rather not be wet. Fortunately for them, science has discovered magical fabrics that can "draw wetness away from the body," so that, frankly, they can pee all day long and never have that uncomfortable chafing that once led so many human beings to the potty chair. Heck, society now offers disposal diapers they can operate themselves—things called Pull-Ups—so that they don't even need you there for the complex maneuver of taping.

I personally don't see what the incentive is for being toilet trained anymore, unless you can persuade them there's some social stigma to remaining steeped in urine all day. This is tricky to accomplish while maintaining their precious self-esteem at the same time. You have to do a kind of tightwire dance of "Yes, of course *I* think you're the most

marvelous human being there is and perfect in every way—
but the nursery school teacher is going to expel your little
behind out of that school if you don't start using the toilet
with the rest of the children!" I admit this is a delicate idea
to get across without doing some possible psychological
damage. (Probably it's a good idea not to be overheard by
mental health professionals or nursery school teachers
when you're speaking of such things.)

Luckily for the human race, most kids finally do get
around to making up their minds to use the toilet on a more
or less regular basis, no matter if you have threatened them
or not. It's something that nature takes care of finally, for
no discernible reason. Just when you're starting to look in
the grocery store for those diapers that advertise "for babies
one hundred pounds and over," one day your child an-
nounces that henceforth such despicable infant products
are not to be brought into the house. Period.

One of my three children decided on a Tuesday morning that she would no longer require the use of diapers and,
unbeknownst to me, threw them all into the trash moments
before the garbage truck came and hauled them away.

"But what about night?" I cried. "You might still be wet
at night, when you're sleeping."

She gave me a look I will never forget: the equivalent of
someone who's just been asked if she believes in capital punishment for babies. "I will *not* be wet at night!" she said,
pulling herself up to her full thirty inches of dignity. "I am
a *dry child!*"

You hate to discourage such conviction in the very
young—but having had children before, I knew that *wanting*
to be dry often isn't quite enough to keep the bed sheets
protected. But in this case, Dry Child turned out to be right.
Of course, that's due to the Midnight Dangle, which all parents of three-year-olds learn to perfect. The Midnight Dangle is when you get up in the middle of the night and hold

your sound-asleep child over the toilet and whisper, "Okay, pee! Come on, let it rip!" until finally, without ever once opening her eyes, the child goes to the bathroom.

In the early days of toilet training, the Midnight Dangle may also have to be expanded to the 2:00 A.M. Dangle, the 2:45 Dangle, the 3:15 Dangle—and so on, until the alarm clock rings and another non-sleeping night can blessedly come to an end. Your co-workers will be vastly amused to hear that you were *dangling* all night and that's why you keep falling asleep at your desk.

At this stage of life, it's helpful to remember two things: one, they all *do* grow up and go off to live dry lives eventually, and two—well, I forget what the second thing is. I think it had something to do with laundry, but honestly I can't remember.

Toothbrushes and other criminals

Hardly anybody thinks about toothbrushes more than three-year-olds. Dentists will beam with pride when you tell them how fascinated your child is with dental hygiene, and will say that this is the ideal time to promote brushing the teeth as a really fun and healthful practice that will stand them in good stead all their lives. Let a dentist get started on this line of talk, and pretty soon you are hearing about plaque and gingivitis and so on down to periodontal troubles in the elderly, who presumably didn't have a love affair with the toothbrush when they were three.

Naturally all this talk doesn't impress a three-year-old very much. They love toothbrushes because early on they discern that these are devices that have personalities that need to be drawn out. Toothbrushes, to someone who is three, are no different from dolls or Legos. In fact, come to think of it, they're kind of like a cross *between* a doll and a Lego, obviously crying out for a dramatic role in the family's life. And even a three-year-old can see that the toothbrushes' personalities can't be illuminated in the few minutes each day that one spends brushing. In fact, using them in an actual human mouth is perhaps the least interesting thing that can be done with them.

· For years, our family's toothbrushes were involved in what we now see was a complicated witness protection program. They were moved from one location to another and handed over to us only when we had reached third-stage anger (this is the stage where our fangs sprout, veins bulge, and language becomes unintelligible). Finally, frustrated with the nightly search for our toothbrushes while our three-year-old was asleep, my husband and I bought secret toothbrushes, which we kept stashed in his briefcase for those nights when we couldn't bear to look in the toy box or behind the dryer one more time.

A lot of people would say this was wimpish of us, that as parents, we had the responsibility to Set Limits and make sure that our child understood that certain things were not to be tolerated. I hear people saying this kind of thing all the time; there's a regular Limit Setting epidemic in this country, if you ask me. And I would like to make it clear that we did say, often and forcefully, "The toothbrushes will remain in the bathroom. They are not to be taken away. They are not toys."

I don't know why it didn't work for us. We managed to keep our children from running into the street by using that same tone of voice. We even got them to quit standing up in their chairs at the dinner table or flinging themselves off the back of the couch, simply by speaking in a now-I-mean-it voice. But children know that you can't possibly enforce everything, and even they can see that toothbrush kidnapping is not a crime you're going to kill them over. After each episode of Forceful Talking on the subject of toothbrushes, the brushes would perhaps stay in their holders for another day or two, and then would mysteriously be spirited off to new homes—under the couch perhaps, or in the riding toys in the backyard. I would not be surprised, even today, to discover a toothbrush jumping out at me from anywhere: the car's glove compartment, under the back stairs, or even hiding out in the winter boots. Some of our brushes became such good pals to our child that they were given names; one beautiful turquoise one was known as Falla Coleria and was said to have a beautiful voice. Another, a red one, was a cowboy named Jack who, I was told, taught school when he wasn't hanging around in the bathroom.

Still, things did get out of hand. Even I will admit this was not an ideal life. One day we were at the veterinarian's office, and the enterprising vet was displaying his supply of doggie toothbrushes and meat-flavored dog toothpaste, trying to persuade me that dog gingivitis was something I should be worrying about. My three-year-old leaped into the air and begged me to get the dog a toothbrush. The vet was surprised, but pleased, to see this notion of dental hygiene being taken up by a mere tot. It looked like a sure sale.

But even I could see that brushing the dog's teeth was not something I'd be able to fit into my life for years to come, and I'm afraid I started laughing rather hysterically at the image of me tracking down the dog and then sitting on his chest while I pried his jaws open and brushed his teeth. What was going to be next, flossing for dogs? Mouthwash for the hamster?

My child, meanwhile, had gone into full-scale meltdown over this. "Mommy, please," he kept begging, and I half expected the vet to join in at any moment, both of them groveling in front of me. "Mommy," screamed my child at last, "don't you care that Falla Coleria and Jack need a pet?"

"Sweetie," I said. "Falla Coleria and Jack have to move

so often that a doggie toothbrush would only get in their way. People like them had to give up the luxury of pets when they went into that program."

The vet was staring at me, so I said to him, "Falla Coleria and Jack are our toothbrushes, you see." Then, because he looked so confused, I added helpfully, "The *people* tooth-brushes."

"What?" he said. "You *named* them?"

"We had to," I said. "It's the only way we can call for them to come back when it's time to use them. But, no matter what you say, I do not think they should have a pet toothbrush."

The kid fell to the floor in a purple rage. The vet backed away, until he made it safely to the door and re-membered he had several hundred things he had to do in the next room.

Creative dressing: "This is what my public expects"

I see three-year-olds all the time wearing shirts, pants, shoes and socks, just like the rest of the human race, and I simply marvel at the good fortune of anyone who has such an agreeable little child in their possession. Many of us have not been so lucky. We are in the company of little children who wouldn't consider going anywhere without, say, a fast-food bucket on the head and perhaps a gray sock worn on the right hand.

I once overheard a woman talking to her three-year-old son, explaining in a fast-food restaurant that the bucket that his hamburger had been served in really had been techni-cally designed for scooping up things at the beach—really not so much as a head adornment.

"Feel how tight it is under the chin?" she said. "That's

because this is the handle that you carry it with, not a chin strap."

He looked away for a long time, taking this information in. We all waited. Finally he said, "That not true. It has Winnie-the-Pooh on it, like the same as my pajamas. You 'posed to wear it."

And sure enough, when she left with him, he was cheerfully wearing his bucket on his head. All the other little kids in the restaurant put their buckets on their heads as well, and one of them was also struggling to mangle a hamburger while wearing a gray sock on his hand.

"He thinks he looks cool with this on," his mother whispered to me. "It's been three weeks now, and all he can say is that it's good on him. Now I suppose there'll be the bucket, too, as part of his outfit."

I don't know why this happens. No one does. All I can figure is that when you're three, you get a sense of fashion. After all, three is a time in your life when you are saying a lot of "why nots" in addition to all the "whys" you're having to ask all the time, and you soon realize that, as the bizarre singer Boy George once expressed it so succinctly, there's enough people dressing ordinary in the world, and why contribute to that?

For a three-year-old, almost anything can be considered an adornment. All the usual stuff is good, of course: the necklaces and bracelets and Christmas ornaments you might find around the house, of course, but why not go way out and insist on wearing one of your father's ties wrapped several times around your waist? Or—and what adult would ever come up with this?—my friend Jennie's daughter felt she was not fully dressed unless she had a wreath of white toilet paper swaddling her neck. She looked rather like she was packed for shipping.

It's difficult to argue with someone's fashion sense, especially when someone is three years old and very possibly a lunatic—but if you are smart, you will hide items that you really don't wish to see being worn out in public. (Hard to keep the toilet paper hidden away at all times, though.) And, of course, the trouble is that you might not be able to tell in advance just which articles might be pressed into wardrobe duty. Who would imagine that Daddy's faded and torn Black Sabbath T-shirt, belted with the dog's leash, will be the Outfit of Choice for the next two weeks? Or that the lovely colorful stickers saying "I Gave Blood—Be Nice to Me" make such a cute statement when plastered all over the cheeks?

My friend Diana had a three-year-old who really should have been employed designing costumes in Hollywood or on Broadway. Too bad the child labor laws are so strict. It was Jessica who first discovered how ominous someone could look, day after day, wearing a red plastic 101 Dalmatians raincoat accessorized with a dog flea collar and the pig-nose mask from Halloween. We all watched breathlessly as new and wonderful items were added to the ensemble during the month it was in vogue for Jessica. At one point she felt the outfit called for one fuzzy bunny bedroom slipper and one yellow plastic boot, then with strands of beads and fake pearls, and then—this was a masterful touch that I particularly applauded—with a purple feather duster poking out of the pocket.

Three-year-old girls, in particular, seem to see dressing for the artistic endeavor it really is. Go into any good daycare center or nursery school, and you'll find the Dramatic Play Area filled with little girls balancing pieces of net on their heads and calling themselves brides. If the day-care center for some reason hasn't stocked up on net, it doesn't matter. Pieces of toilet paper can be pressed into service as veils. In fact, my daughter once confided to me that she preferred toilet paper veils to the "real" kind because you could make the toilet paper kind as long as you wanted.

"And," she said, "if the teacher isn't looking, you can even wrap yourself all the way up in the toilet paper and then the dress matches the veil." I'm just hoping she'll be this easygoing when it comes time to select a *real* wedding dress and veil.

Boys are also not immune to the lure of dressing to impress. Although many of them go through an alarming stage where they want eye shadow and gowns with sequins, by the time they're three most of them have sorted out the fact that this is cumbersome clothing, and that eye shadow is difficult to apply, especially when other people are screaming at you that it's not appropriate. Most of the three-year-old boys you encounter have even been willing to give up the three-inch spiked high heels they find in the back of their mother's closet.

But this is not to say they have no style. Mainly what happens with boys is they find an outfit that makes them feel incredibly handsome and sexy—and then they insist on wearing it until it falls apart, thread by thread, on their bodies, or until their body parts start to rot underneath it, whichever comes first. Some of them, unhappily, never grow out of this stage.

But no matter what the clothing fetish is—anything from the sock on the hand to the toilet paper necklace or the cowboy hat—if you ask, "Why do you wear that every day?" the answer is always the same: "It good on me."

How do you spell "independence"? I DO IT

Somehow, programmed into the brain cells of most little kids is the confidence that they are capable of running the whole world. I don't know quite where they get this idea— surely it's not that we adults, rushing around all the time and screaming at intermittent intervals, make it look easy.

But as we all know, unless we're talking about the United States Congress, they probably can't run it any better than we've done. You can try to explain it to them again and again: three-year-olds are employable as clowns, fashion consultants, and possibly demolition experts—but other than that, there's still a lot of skills they need to brush up on, or acquire for the first time.

How is it that a person who can't even see over the top of the dining room table feels herself ready and able to assume the role of Dictator of the House? Where *do* they get the notion that they are the bosses of all they survey? I think it's just another of nature's cruel jokes, that little people get the desire to be the boss of everything long before they can even hold a spoon.

But where does this leave you, the hapless parent? As usual, you're the one who has to break the bad news: no one under the height of three and a half feet is going to be allowed to use the stove. And besides that, the kitty will *never* be put in the oven, no matter how cold we think the kitty is. "No kitty," you hear yourself saying, "is ever happy going into the oven."

Suddenly, now that you're the handler of a three-year-old dictator-in-training, everything is just slightly more of a fight than you're ready for. Getting dressed in the morning becomes like a triathlon. You can set out your child's clothes the night before, thinking you're going to save time—but how could you have predicted that only green clothes will be worn from now on? You didn't know. And what's that hang-up you have with pants having to zip up in the front and tags in the back? You discover that you really are a shockingly conventional person when it comes to apparel.

Then, when you step forward to help your little one get dressed, with only three minutes to spare before the two of you are supposed to walk out the door, you will find yourself met with a wall of outraged resistance. "I WILL DO IT!"

your child screams, and then in case you didn't understand that perfectly well, *"I WILL DO IT! Get away from me!"*

Why does this happen? Who knows, unless it's just to show that Mother Nature has a sense of humor and loves practical jokes? All you know is that you could have had his shirt buttoned in five and a half seconds, but it's taken him twenty tearful minutes, and it's still buttoned up wrong— but somehow if you move even one nostril hair closer to him, he drops to the floor and screams once again, "I DO IT! I DO IT! I DO IT!"

So here's what you have to get used to: When you are living with a person of this age, you will constantly be sus- pected of trying to keep this person from his rightful place as Ruler of the World. My youngest child announced when she was three years old that she was the King. She would say this in the threatening voice you sometimes hear on television shows, like when the criminal shouts out, "Stand back! I have a knife!" Picture him yelling, "Stand back! I the King!" and you've got the approximate idea of the sense of menace involved here.

Once, smiling, I asked if she didn't mean that she was the Queen instead, since she was a girl and all. But somehow she'd already ascertained that Kings outweigh Queens in the power department, and she was quite sure she wasn't going to mess around being second place. "I the King," she growled.

I don't know what it's like over in Buckingham Palace, but I found living with a King to be a tiresome proposition. I'd have cut her peeled apple into appropriate wedges, and she'd screech at me that there was a speck of peel still re- maining, and Kings didn't *eat* peelings. I would sometimes argue that a person, even a royal one, had to be adaptable enough to tolerate a little apple peel here and there, that it was going to be a long, unhappy life indeed if one allowed oneself to be stopped dead by one itsy bitsy sliver of *edible* peel on a wedge of apple—but believe me, this is an argument that's difficult to win. At best, by the end of it, both of you will be furious and screaming—and because you are bigger (and may even *be* the King—of the house, at least), the little one will be sent to her room, and you will be gnashing your teeth and wishing you'd just cut the damned piece of apple correctly while you still had a shred of your sanity intact.

One day when we were going through that bit about her being the King, I said to her, "We depose Kings around here. Here's a piece of apple, go and play for a while because I have to cook supper." I said it three more times, too—once when there was a question of the ethics of washing a King's ears, and another time when the legality of putting an actual King to bed came up.

To my surprise, each time she accepted the verdict—but then in the middle of the night, there she was by my bedside.

"What is it?" I said, after I realized that that slow tapping on my shoulder meant that someone wanted a 3:00 A.M. conversation.

"I want to know something," she said in a wide-awake voice. "What means that thing you said?"

This is a horrible question to be asked in the middle of the night, and I had to think for a very long time. Hadn't I just that day drawn the line on eating any more matchsticks? Was she recalling the moment I said that Jack the Toothbrush couldn't teach morning classes before Daddy had a chance to brush his teeth? What? What?

"About Kings," she said. "You said about Kings."

"Oh, deposed. Kings are deposed. That means no more Kings. This is America, and we only had Elvis for a King, but he's not around anymore."

"Where he go?"

"No one's really sure," I said. (One of my firm child-rearing rules is that you don't want to bring up death in the middle of the night if you can possibly get around it.) "Tomorrow I'll play you a song from the King, and then you'll see you're really *you* and not the King."

I suppose that, when you stop and think about it, a child with a developing psyche might really need to try out the idea that she really is the ruler of the whole world, the beacon that all of us have been waiting to steer by. I mean, it's something worth trying out for as long as you can—you know, yell it out a few times, and see how many subjects you can recruit.

But sometimes—and this is useful information to know—when they're three, you can still confuse them, and for a moment at least, they go back to sleep.

Scenes in public now that they can tell people how rotten you are

Some people weren't told before they became parents that they would have to leave the whole idea of dignity at the door. This is information that I feel legally should be distributed to everyone, perhaps starting in the elementary school years but definitely by high school. I'm sure our parents tried to tell us, but they were too hysterical to make much sense—and besides that, we all wanted babies. We just didn't understand that one of those days the baby was going to grow up and come walking out of our bedroom with our stained and disgusting underwear on their heads—while company is over. *Of course* company is over when this happens. Where would the fun be of just doing such a performance for the immediate family?

And, okay, it's not just the underpants thing either. They also tell things about you: that you picked your nose in the car the other day, for instance, and that you mash on the gas when the light turns yellow—and they'll stand up in church to share the fact that in the morning your breath smells like poop.

Oh, it's a whole wacky, wonderful world when they learn to talk. Those little keen baby eyes that have been observing you for three years now have a mouthpiece working on their behalf—and they're only too happy to innocently share anything they feel should be reported to the public at large.

Take my friend Lillie, for instance. She sat by, mortified, when Delilah, her three-year-old, announced at dinner with Lillie's in-laws that Mommy had dropped the turkey on the floor, and then had said, "Shit, nobody's sober enough to care."

You might be as amazed as Lillie was that a three-year-old could come out with such a perfect mimicry of that sentence—but Delilah managed just fine, thank you. She even managed a cruel little smile when she said the word "sober," just as Lillie had probably done minutes before.

Lillie hasn't decided which fact was more incriminating: the turkey droppage itself, the swear word, or the fact that she was calling her mother-in-law the kind of lush who couldn't tell the difference between an intact turkey and one that had gone sliding across the floor on its backside. At any rate, the rest of the meal did not go well, and the in-law relationship hasn't been that great lately either.

Three-year-olds also have a love affair with words like "poop" and "pee" and "boogers," and they will bring these subjects up at every opportunity—and even sometimes when there's not really an opportunity but they've just invented one. My three-year-old once announced to an entire fast-food restaurant that the hamburger she just ate reminded her of poop and the orange soda tasted like pee.

She was saying, "And the little things on the hamburger bun are boo—" when we tackled her and dragged her outside. I remember she looked amazed. "Those were my jokes!" she said. "People liked it!"

They are constantly tuned in to any subject that's likely to be the most embarrassing for as many people as possible. Once my friend Anna was in the video store when her child shrieked with joy: "Mommy, look! Some dorfs are here! Mommy, dorfs! Snow White might come!"

Anna busied herself searching for something on the bottom shelf, so that she could crouch in the fetal position and pray to disappear altogether. But Madeleine was not to be discouraged, in keeping with the three-year-old's creed of never letting anything go until all parties are completely exhausted and/or humiliated.

"Mommy, there's dorfs here! Mommy, come look at the dorfs! Do you know where Snow White is? Do you know where Snow White is, dorfs? Mommy, come look at the dorfs! They are so cute!"

Anna managed somehow to choose a video, pay for it, and get out of the store with her faculties still intact. She says she apologized to the short people, the video store customers, and the universe dozens of times.

"I'm sorry," she said. "She's *three*."

Come to think of it, that's the reason for a lot of things that are going to happen to you during that last toddler year. You'll be reciting this like a mantra: "She's three. She's three. She's three." After which you'll say, "I'm sorry. I'm sorry. I'm sorry."

Things They Tell Everyone About You

- You don't have enough money to buy all the toys in the store.
- You don't really recycle; you throw nearly everything in the garbage.
- You never dust.
- You said a really terrible word last night.
- You press down on the gas pedal when the light is yellow.
- You take a pill so you won't have any more babies.
- You dye your hair because it's getting too gray.
- You think you're fat.
- You actually are fat.

Ranking scale of tantrums

Tantrums intensify when your kid gets to be three. This is unfortunate because by now your child isn't so little that you can heave him up over your shoulder and be off down the street, whistling nonchalantly. A three-year-old child dissolving into a tantrum can rip your throat out with his bared teeth, and can dig his fingernails into your scalp so hard that your brain cells recoil and try to regroup in other parts of your body. And his screams and shrieks can easily shatter the glass on storefront windows for miles, as well as gain the interest of any number of public officials.

It's helpful, I think, to know the ranking system for tantrums, just as it is with hurricanes. A Stage One tantrum, of course, can become Stage Four in a matter of minutes, so you may want to gather your wits about you and evacuate when you see the beginnings of one brewing.

Here's what to look for:

STAGE ONE: Voice is raised in an irritating whine, but child remains in upright position. May tell you that your breath smells bad and that you look stupid in your new coat. Starts to repeat same thing over and over again: "Mommy, please! Mommy, please! Mommy, please!" works, as does an emphatic, "No! No! No! No! No!"

Onlooker reaction: Most will ignore and go about their business.

Your reaction: Reasoning with child. Communicating kind- ness and good intentions, along with appropriate firmness.

STAGE TWO: Child is now definitely screaming. Eyes are bulging, spittle is flying around. May stamp foot and clench fists. Says she doesn't like you anymore, that you are no longer her mommy and can't attend any birthday festivities planned. Not only that, Santa Claus will be informed about your transgressions, as well as Daddy, Grandma, and the people at your work.

Onlooker reaction: People look a little surprised but try to hurry past. So far, no cell phone activity discernible. Probably they are not intending to call the police.

Your reaction: You try to pick up your child and speak in a soothing voice. You hope all the strangers notice your kind eyes and the fact that you haven't hit the child. Voice a little more firm, but still pleasant.

STAGE THREE: Screams, tears, shouts, threats—anything that will work. Kid falls to the floor in a rage, kicks, flails arms. Now claims to hate you and all you have ever done or said. May even become a chant: "I hate you! I hate you! I hate you!" Flings body on floor if you try to approach. Pulls away, runs into traffic when you come near.

Onlooker response: People look alarmed and as though they are trying to decide whether or not to intervene. Some will ask the child if he's all right—as if he's the one in need of solace and not you.

Your response: Pick up the kid and get the hell out of there as fast as possible.

STAGE FOUR: Turning into a regular meltdown. High-pitched shrieks replace the previous screams and shouts. Obviously the forces of darkness are being called upon to destroy you and your pitiful, hideous lifestyle and ideas. Child may start to bang head on the floor or hold breath, will lunge at you to bite your face off—anything to frighten you and anyone else. Ear protection and helmets necessary for those standing close by.

Onlooker response: People now obviously rushing to your child's aid. You expect police officers and social service agency people to come and lead you away into a squad car.

Your response: Hoping the squad car gets there soon and that the foster mother knows what she's in for.

2
At Day Care,
They Call Me Batman

Day care: an idea whose time has come

Say what you will about feeling guilty for letting someone else take care of your child—by the time most kids turn three, they are anxious to rule more kingdoms than you can provide in your own home. If they didn't start day care as babies, it's evident that now they need to go to one as soon as possible, just so they can extend their range of bossiness. Managing you, the dog, and the toothbrushes isn't enough anymore. They need other people, and there's hardly anybody better to practice on than other three-year-olds, who are also practicing on them.

It sounds good in theory—the whole day-care system—but I'm sorry to tell you that this, like a lot of other things about parenting, is going to be a little bit traumatic for you. There are moments you will wake up in a cold sweat in the middle of the night, remembering in excruciating detail every day-care horror story you've ever heard. And new horror stories will spring up every day on the news, too; pretty soon it will be clear to you that 98 percent of the children in day-care centers are in mortal danger, that day-care workers across America have mostly been recruited from prison farms.

That is how it will feel, but I beg you to remember that

most day-care centers are staffed by earnest Early Childhood Educators who do not carry weapons and do not have grudges against little people. They, in fact, are delighted to watch your child for several hours each day, and best of all, they don't even think you're a bad person for not wanting to do this yourself. They understand your need to be out in the world among people who are not discussing poop at the top of their lungs.

So, after interviewing forty-seven day-care providers and watching out for telltale catch phrases such as "corporal punishment" and "discipline by negative reinforcement," you select a lovely center that has a fenced-in yard, shady trees, smiling teachers, and a policy that specifically states they don't toss children in the trash bin.

Your child will not be amazingly grateful for this right at first. In fact, he will probably scream every day when it appears you intend to drop him there. He will not only scream but he'll cling pitifully to your leg, begging to be taken back home. After his first week there, he'll tell you the Class Bad Boy steps on his toes every single day, and that the other kids put boogers on his plate at snack time, and that the teacher has bad breath. Life is simply unlivable at day care; it's intolerable, untenable, not to be borne, and besides that, the other kids always make him be a dog in the Dramatic Play Area, and he doesn't know how to bark like a "real doggie."

Your brain will shut down upon hearing the information that there are known Bad Boys in the day-care system, and it will most likely be several hours before the rest of the message gets through, namely that nasal excrement is being shown to your own dear child, and that—yikes!—he's also being made to bark like a dog for other people. Suddenly his life will appear to you like a sequel to *Lord of the Flies*, or the nursery school version of *Natural Born Killers*.

Just as you are ready to forfeit your deposit and first

month's tuition, inform the authorities, and keep your child at home until he's in his mid-thirties, the world shifts. Suddenly he loves being there. The most amazingly wonderful people are in that classroom every day. The toys there are the best in the world, he's learned a really great bark, and best of all, he's learned to *love* the idea of boogers and snacks.

Now he saves his weeping for Saturdays and Sundays when, unfortunately, the place isn't open, and he has to be with you. He will sorrowfully point to the calendar at home, sniffling over the fact that the days at the beginning and the end of each row are something he calls "home days."

"Home days are when you have to stay with Mommy and Daddy, even if you don't want to," he'll say to you.

And you'll say, "Thanks, day care."

Who is this person I gave birth to?

There's more news about day care, I'm afraid. Your kid won't be going there even one week when you notice that she's assumed a completely different identity. I'll never forget the day the nursery school director pulled me aside and said in a concerned whisper, "Your daughter has told us that her real name is Nixie, but we've checked on all the forms, and we were sort of curious as to why *you* didn't tell us her real name."

Do you believe this? Her *real name*? I had a momentary impulse to say, "Well, actually we were trying to keep it a secret. Her full name is Nixadocious, but most people think that's a name for the criminally insane, so we just call her Stephanie. But if you want to call her Nixie, I guess the cat's out of the bag."

Instead I said something lame like, "What—?" And then followed up with, "Oh, she's full of imagination, isn't she?"

But from the way the woman was looking at me, I could tell she wasn't really buying it. She was sure that we were closet Nixie-namers. Actually that was when an important fact of life first dawned on me, and you might want to remember this, too: *Day-care teachers and directors believe what our children tell them, even though our children are three years old.*

In addition to making up new names for themselves, they also tell wild stories about what went on at your house last night. And believe me, they are not above a little embroidery. The excuse is, of course, that they're too young to tell fact from fiction, and so we're supposed to not mind too much when they tell the teacher that Daddy gave them a gun for their birthday—"a real one, too. It shoots everybody!"

Back in the '50s, when all parents were incarnations of Ward and June Cleaver or Harriet and Ozzie Nelson, it might have worked to just smile and shrug all this stuff off. But today, for some bizarre reason, little children are widely regarded as the major truth tellers of our time, and parents are seen as possible dope-smuggling ax murderers, filled with deep secrets and untoward impulses.

My friend Cathy has a son who, for a full year, wanted to be called Batman. Perhaps *wanted* is too mild a word. The truth was he wouldn't respond to any name *other* than Batman. He announced this at home, in his nursery school, and out in public. Cathy remembered about half the time that she was dealing with Batman instead of Brian, and was always amazed when he was so capable of ignoring her when she used his real name by accident. But one day they were out together at the grocery store and he was explaining to a man in line that he was named Batman, when the man gave Cathy a strange look, and said, "You parents today! You always give your children such trendy names."

Some theorists think that children need to be corrected every time they assume a false identity so that they don't get the idea that they really *are* Batman. They say we do them a disservice when we allow them to think they've turned into superheroes and that we buy the fact that they aren't ordinary little children anymore.

But I've been watching kids for a while now, and I think they just like to order us around in new and inventive ways. If they can convince us to reorder our brain cells to think of them as some other name, then they get extra points in the ongoing Kid-Parent Contest. And that's worth everything.

The uses of a one-eyed bunny and a stack of cotton balls

One thing that no parent is ever prepared for is the introduction of a new love object—a parent substitute, as it were. Once it becomes clear that you don't intend to hang out with your child twenty-four hours a day, seven days a week, he realizes that he's going to have to find something he can count on to be more permanent than you are. And he picks something nearby—a stuffed animal or blanket, if you're lucky, or the electric drill, if you're not.

My friend Lisa had to take to her bed in grief the first time her child fell asleep clutching his one-eyed, stuffed gray bunny instead of insisting that *she* stay with him until he fell asleep.

"He doesn't need me anymore! I've been replaced," she kept wailing.

I knew how she felt, but that *is* the point of parenthood, after all: to gradually become less and less necessary, until finally your child can make his own way in the world. Someday he'll not only be able to fall asleep without you there but he also may insist on living in another state, going to a job with people you never meet, and asking you not to call him before 9:00 A.M. on Saturday mornings because he and *his wife* like to sleep late.

And besides all that, it's worth remembering that even if a one-eyed gray bunny can assist in getting the kid to go to sleep, you're still the one who's needed to put the Band-Aids on and cook the macaroni and cheese. The stuffed animal business hasn't progressed that far yet.

Still, it's tough to take in when they're still three years old, and you realize a piece of yellow fleece sewn up to look like a duckling with a hat can take *your* place. It may take a few days before you can truly congratulate yourself that you don't have to sit by the bed for four hours waiting for your child's REM sleep to subside so you can tiptoe out of the room.

Sociologically speaking, it's always interesting to see what kids choose as their "love" objects. You can try to direct this process as much as possible—steer her toward a lovely sleek pink hippopotamus that's fully washable and can even go into the dryer. But chances are, it's going to be something that's not quite so convenient. My friend Ellie had a kid who became attached to an extension cord that had been attached to their Christmas tree lights. Ellie ended up having to cut off the plug end so that Matthew could sit and fondle the cord for as long as he wanted, without risk of electrocution.

Another, luckier, friend had a kid who carried around a stack of cotton balls that he referred to as his kitties. He would suck his thumb while rubbing a cotton ball on his nose. This, I think, is about as ideal a love object as you're going to find in this lifetime—and even though his mother didn't think it up for him, she should have. You might want to try to introduce cotton balls to your own kid in search of a love object. After all, cotton balls never go bad, the world makes so many of them that you never hear about a shortage, and best of all, when they get dirty and disgusting, you can throw them away and replace them without your child ever figuring out that his One Special Beloved Cotton Ball kitty is gone.

My friend Linda had a kid who had a Linus-type blanket that he dragged around with him all the time. Predictably, it became the source for many of the diseases of the Western Hemisphere as it traveled through mud puddles, parking lots, and the restroom of gas stations and hardware stores. Since Michael couldn't envision himself going even one minute without this blanket, Linda was not allowed to wash it except in the middle of the night when he was in fourth-stage sleep and when *she* was too tired to remember where the washing machine was anyway.

That's when she embarked on an ingenious plan. Rather than try to talk Michael out of this love object—which never works and probably causes extensive psychological damage that you'll be hearing about from guidance counselors up into the high school years—Linda simply started going into Michael's room every night and snipping off a piece of the blanket. She cut off such a small portion that later she described it as "shaving" the blanket.

He never knew, of course. That's how great she was at this. And she would hide the blanket dust—because that's what it really was, it was so small a piece—in the bottom of the kitchen garbage can each night, so that he would never know.

She did this for years. It became a bedtime ritual for her. You know: 1, Brush teeth. 2, Floss. 3, Shave blanket.

And by the time Michael entered first grade, the blanket fit neatly inside his front pocket—and he was none the wiser.

Friends, that's what a little patience can do.

You are belly button lint, and the teacher is a goddess

If you have survived your child's toddlerhood, you might be under the impression that you are an okay person and are deserving of all the unconditional love your child has thus far bestowed upon you. After all, who knows better than you the precise way to kiss a boo-boo to make things better? And who talks like Donald Duck better than you? And haven't your brain cells been conditioned to jump to attention from a sound sleep the second that your child so much as tosses in his sleep and murmurs "Mama"?

Yes, by the time your child is three, you have completely morphed into a High-Caliber Parent. Oh, sure, there was the unfortunate day you went off to answer the phone and your kid tumbled down the stairs. You were sure the authorities would be at the door to escort him to his new foster home where some perfect parents were awaiting him. But by the time the week was out and the cops still hadn't shown up to take him, you relaxed a bit. You'd gotten away with it. At some point it occurs to you that the state's too busy to go after every parent who talks on the phone when there's a toddler in the house. And anyway, you have to admit you've done a wonderful job of transforming yourself into someone whose every waking thought is somehow tied up with this new human being. Why, you hardly miss things from your old life anymore: sleeping past 7:00 A.M., reading the newspaper, flossing your teeth.

All I can say is, you are in for a rude awakening when your child starts day care or nursery school.

Your time of being the World's Most Important Person is drawing to an end. It's not that your wonderfulness has vanished. You still have many sterling qualities—and in a pinch, you'll do. But suddenly you're hearing about this *teacher* all the time, and it turns out that for every decent thing you've ever done, she's done lots more. She has made a lifetime of superb deeds, while you were merely getting by.

One day when I picked my child up from day care she said to me nonchalantly, "How many worms have you saved today?"

I knew I was in trouble, because I have never knowingly saved even one worm. I don't even particularly *like* worms, although I have to admit they are not as bad as some other animals I could mention. The only thing that makes them okay at all in my book is that they do something good for the soil, something I can't right now remember what it is— and also I've never heard of an instance of a worm biting anyone, although maybe it happened and I just wasn't told.

But there we were, with the question on the table: exactly how many worms had I saved that day?

I believe basically in being honest with children, so I said I had not saved one worm.

"Hmmm," she said. "Maria saved five worms."

"That's good," I said. I wanted to point out that when you're walking around outside with slow-pokey *toddlers*, for God's sake, you could afford to spend some time looking for worms to save. In fact, you would probably have to do something like that to keep from losing your mind. Others of us, I wanted to mention, were in offices, where the worm population was not so much in evidence.

Instead I said, "Maria is a very nice person."

"Why you not save any worms, too?"

"My boss is kind of a stickler about this kind of thing," I said. "When I'm at work, he really feels as though I should stay there working, and not go out in the parking lot looking for worms to save."

"Your boss not nice."

"Well, he's nice"—I remembered to put this in, or the

next time the Boss and the Kid met up, the Kid would be sure to mention it—"but he's paying me to write stories on the computer, and not to save worms."

"Maria says everybody should care about worms."

"I'm sure my boss cares a great deal about worms. I know he does, but when we're at work, other people have to take care of the worms."

"Maria take care of the worms."

"I know that."

There was a long silence, and I turned on the radio, hoping we were done. But after a few minutes she said, "On home days, you not save worms."

Later I wanted to call Maria and tell her to stop it with the worms already, and give the rest of us a break. But my husband didn't think it would be a good idea. Let her save worms, he said. It's good that our kids think other people in the world do nice things. We don't have to be *everything* to her.

It was a beautiful sentiment, and I think he felt that way for fifteen whole minutes, which was when our daughter fell and refused to let him put a Band-Aid on her boo-boo because, she said, he didn't know how to do it right.

"Maria put a Band-Aid on and your boo-boo gets all better right then," she said.

It must be all that worm juice on her fingers, I told him.

The red cup and other day-care social conundrums

As the parent of a kid in day care, you will learn that your child's life there revolves around a few simple concepts:

- Red cups are the only kind worth having at snack time.
- If a kid at day care says that today he is a dog, not

only does *he* have to bark but you have to bark
back to communicate with him.

• Being a dog at day care is very, very cool.

• If somebody does something truly wicked to you—
like steal your red cup—the very best revenge is
to tell him he can't come to your birthday party.
This will demoralize him for days, even if your
birthday isn't coming up for another eleven
months.

• Teachers at day care say you have to use your
words and not slug anybody, but no matter how
much you *say* you always have to have the red cup,
they will not always give it to you.

• It's not the same to bring your own red cup from
home.

It's astonishing, really, to see that life can be organized
around such few principles. But, of course, there are aux-
iliary rules and regulations that must be followed—and the
average three-year-old picks them up in a snap. They have
to. Their whole social life and reputation depend upon it.
People imagine that little children are simply stacking
blocks or rocking baby dolls to sleep, but every now and
then, if you're lucky, you get a little glimpse into what their
real lives are like at day care.

One day, for instance, my daughter was getting dressed
for day care, and since the laundry was just done, I proudly
produced her very favorite shirt, the one with cutout fuzzy
bears.

"Oh, I can't wear that anymore," she said.

"But why? You love this shirt!" The week before, the
main problem had been that I insisted she couldn't wear it
every day because most of the time it was covered with peanut butter, red punch, Play-Doh, and the occasional blob of
oatmeal.

"Everybody has to touch it all day long, and if you say no, they get mad at you," she said.

"They want to touch your shirt?" I said.

"The fuzzy part," she told me. "And I tell them no, only Cara and Matthew can touch the fuzzy part today, but it doesn't matter. They run up to me and do it anyway. Katie hit me because I said no."

"Why only Cara and Matthew?"

"Well." She gave me the look that meant a long, convoluted explanation was coming, one she doubted I could really follow. "Matthew was nice to me and let me kiss him one day, and Cara told me I could be her kitty when I grow up."

"Be her kitty when you grow up? But you're not going to be anybody's kitty when you grow up—you're going to be a human being. You'll be a woman."

"I'm not going to be a woman."

"I don't think you get a choice. It will just happen."

She shook her head sadly. "Nope. I'm going to be a kitty and live at Cara's house. She said I could live there if I let her touch my shirt."

"And what about Matthew?"

"I kiss him." She giggled. "He's thinking now if he wants to be a boy kitty and get married to me. I ask him every day."

I wasn't sure how to break the news to my husband later that evening that (1) our daughter had gone into business selling the rights to touch her shirts, and (2) the price of a shirt touch was either a kiss or an offer of housing, and (3) she hoped to change species, and (4) was actively pursuing a boy and trying to convince him to change species also and marry her.

Instead, I just told him she needed some new clothes, and quietly bought her some plain, non-fuzzy, no-teddy-bears pullover shirts. Later she told me that Matthew had made up his mind to stay a human boy, and that Cara's mother said they already had too many cats anyway, and she was ready to wear the fuzzy shirt again.

"So I'm going to stay here with Daddy," she said.

"And you'll grow up and be a woman?"

"Yes," she said. "But where are you going to live when Daddy and I get married?"

Speaking of Daddy...

Yes, you are the mommy, and yes, you are said to be the most important person in your child's little universe. You know this is true because, first of all, all the books say so, and besides that, you must be important since all the parenting experts blame you when things go wrong. But most tellingly, it's *you* who has the satisfaction of being the one who gets screamed for when its 2:30 A.M. and your child thinks the Winnie-the-Pooh lamp is doubling as a marauding monster that spiders are crawling on.

So why is it that the artwork your child does at day care always shows you looking like a toad?

At first you say to yourself, "Well, it's just that she doesn't know how to draw so well, and she didn't mean to depict me with those huge black eyebrows and that scowl. Probably the black crayon was the only one available."

You say this, and you actually believe it. Then two things will probably happen, nearly immediately. You'll find out somehow that the black crayons were *not* so available, that your child, in fact, had to ask for one special, just to get your eyebrows and frown drawn in so darkly. And, as you're taking to your bed to recover from that news, a picture will come home that shows Daddy—golden, smiling Daddy with the sun blooming right over his head and stars glowing around his stick arms.

Even the sun is smiling.

I'm sorry, but it's hard to put this aside and go about your life. It's *real* hard, for instance, when marauding monsters and spiders have again possessed the poor Pooh lamp at 2:30 A.M., and you're bitterly thinking, "Oh, yeah? Why don't you ask Mr. Sunshine on His Head to get down on his knees and chase spiders and monsters for you? Mrs. Dark Eyebrows is a little tiny bit too tired!"

I don't know what to tell you about this Daddy Adoration Phenomenon—either where it comes from or why it's so widespread among little kids. Somehow, even though you're clearly the one putting up with the most of the childhood shenanigans and being the maternal, supportive presence in the house, you don't get the true credit you deserve. Welcome to motherhood.

Sometimes, if you are lucky, Daddy will become so in favor that *he* will be the one called for in the middle of the night, and you'll be allowed to simply roll over and go back to sleep. But even that, you will realize, doesn't help. You lie there in bed, listening to the spider chasing and then hearing the reassurances and good-nights—and believe me, you are not thinking how terrific it is that you are still under your covers. You are thinking, "Why does *he* get to be Mr. Wonderful?"

All I can advise here is to wait it out. The day will come when Mr. Wonderful makes an egregious tactical error. Maybe not today, maybe not even tomorrow. Okay, so maybe it's not until he puts his foot down about taking the car all night long on the evening of the prom—but there you will be, suddenly seen as the divine, inspiring presence you've been all along. It's then that you can say to your child, "Darling, could you just do me one little favor before I allow you to take *my* car to the prom? Would you just draw a little picture of me with the sun over my head and birds chirping all around me—and maybe put Daddy in the background with a big frown?"

Day-care romances

Make no mistake about it. Day-care centers and nursery schools bear a very close resemblance to singles bars. Four-year-olds—and maybe some advanced threes—think about falling in love almost as much as twenty-somethings. While they're sitting in the sandbox, pushing trucks around through the dirt, they are actually plotting romantic strategy, planning weddings, and—alas, in this modern day—even figuring out their divorces and follow-up romances.

My friend Anna's four-year-old son once collapsed in tears at the breakfast table, and all she could get out of him was that some curly-haired girl from day care had said they were getting married, and that was that. This wasn't going to be just a day-care marriage of convenience either—this was the Real Thing.

"And I don't know what I'll do if I meet somebody else!" he wailed.

You really don't want to explain to your little child that this is a problem plaguing humans for thousands of years, so Anna just informed him that he did not have to get married at age four, and that he could continue to see other women for as long as he wished. Then she dried his tears, helped him blow his nose, and sent him off.

It becomes obvious that girls are the ones masterminding this romance stuff, while boys are home sniffling into their corn flakes over their romantic fate. This is something you can't worry about. You may be doing all you can to raise both genders the same, but believe me, girls of four have somehow already figured out that guys can be slow in the Romance Department and that they have to help things along.

Helping things along was what my four-year-old daughter was doing the day she stood in the Dress-up Corner in her wedding veil, screaming to Michael who was trying to play trucks: "Michael, get over here and marry me!"

The teacher, who told me this story, said that Michael kept pushing his truck around, trying to ignore her.

"Michael, you said today we would get married, and it's today!" she yelled.

He made truck noises.

"Michael, my veil is falling off me! Come over here now!"

Louder truck noises.

She regarded him furiously but silently. One of her would-be bridesmaids made her a cup of pretend tea, knowing you need feminine support as well as make-believe chemical sustenance at a distressful time like this. But my daughter, the teacher said, waved the tea away and kept glaring at Michael. Then she drew herself up and delivered the killer blow: "All right, Michael. If you don't come and marry me today, you can't come to my birthday!"

Later, on the way home from day care in the car, my daughter reported that after snack time, they had had a quiet conversation, just the two of them, about their impending wedding, and she had asked him what the problem was.

All he would say was that he would draw her a picture about it that night at home.

"Well, that's a good thing," I told her. "He'll use art to explain it."

She looked doubtful. "I *know* what the problem is," she said. "I can't take the wedding veil out of the Dress-up Corner. He wants to play with trucks in the Truck Corner. How can we get married if we can't stand next to each other?"

"Hmmm," I said. "That *does* sound like a technical hang-up."

"I don't see what a picture could say for *that*," she said. The next day, however, the picture didn't materialize. But it didn't matter. A boy named Sammy was sick of playing with trucks and thought marriage might be just the thing to occupy him for a morning's entertainment. He willingly came over to the Dress-up Corner—a place where not many males had apparently dared to venture—and underwent a wedding ceremony and then was summarily dismissed back to the trucks by the girls.

"So," I said. "You're married to Sammy instead. That's quite a development!"

She sighed and looked out the window. "Well, I had the veil on, so I had to marry somebody."

The things they can do at day care and can't do at home

For reasons no one has been able to figure out, day-care centers know how to get children to be competent in ways that none of the rest of us can manage. For instance, when you peek into the play yard at a day-care center on a cold day, you will see lots of little children outside—and they are all wearing coats!

This, as any mother of a toddler can tell you, is an out-and-out miracle. Toddlers and teenagers do not wear coats, except under court order. To get the average three-year-old to dress appropriately for the weather, you mostly have to be willing to sit on him while you shove his arms into sleeves. This takes a level of athleticism that you may not always have on hand. The first time I saw a class of twenty-four preschoolers outside, riding tricycles and wearing winter clothing, I figured the teachers must have had degrees in martial arts to get so many of them dressed simultaneously. I could imagine them conducting surprise attacks, leaping out from behind bookcases and from underneath tables to tackle their charges and drag them to their outerwear.

But no. If you've ever sat in on a nursery school class, you'll hear the teacher say something like, "Okay, get your outdoor clothing on now," and watch as everybody goes over to the coat rack and then proceeds to *put on a coat.* Children in day care can do this for themselves. It is an inspiring sight, the vision of a bunch of little kids, in synchrony, putting on coats. It's like watching a drill team or something.

They have an interesting method, too. A day-care kid putting on a coat first flings it to the ground, then walks around so that he's standing next to the neckline part, leans down and sticks his arms into the sleeves. (This is the point when you're about to say, "No, no, no, your coat is going to be upside down!" Trust me: you shouldn't.) He then flips the coat over his head, and presto! He's wearing it.

Obviously the payoff for the kid is the wonderful, exhilarating moment when he gets to whip the coat over his head—and all the contents of the pockets, the marbles, the Legos, the dresser drawer knobs, spill out and jangle all over the floor. But this is a small price for a parent to pay in order to get a bunch of children ready to go outside and play. After a few times of this, everybody gets tired of hunting down the dresser knobs, the Legos, and the marbles, and they roll away underneath things and go off to that other universe, never to be heard from again.

Day-care teachers are also masters at getting children to clean up after themselves, something no child has ever done in a family home. I've actually seen whole classes of three-year-olds hard at work stacking blocks, wiping down tables, and putting markers back in their boxes. Once I heard a child in diapers ask the teacher, "What can me clean?" I almost called the television news.

Yet when you ask day-care personnel how they get these miracles to happen, they simply shrug. Once a teacher pulled me aside and said that *parents* could have kids doing these things at home, if they would only take the time to teach children the skills.

"Parents just think it's easier to do everything themselves," she said. "Also, I suspect they're invested in keeping their children small and dependent upon them. They *claim* they want their children to help out, but I believe they really don't."

This is an unfair assumption, of course. We'd be happy to have our children dress themselves rather than make every clothing situation a knock-down-drag-out kick-boxing tournament. We just didn't know you could enter a coat by first throwing it on the floor and whipping it over your head in a sneak attack.

I think teachers have lots of other secrets, too, things they learned in the Teacher College, things that they don't want to share with the rest of us until they feel we're truly ready. How else can we explain the fact that many of them are still smiling at the end of the day?

3
Your Life, Only Interrupted

They didn't mention this in childbirth class, and nobody sure as hell is going to bring it up now (the adoption agencies are already overloaded, and anyway, the authorities are trying to discourage parents from signing up with the merchant marines), but you are never again going to be on time for another thing in your life. Truly organized people will fight against the idea that one tiny child can so alter their existence, but I think that the sooner you accept this, the happier you'll be.

When you are the possessor of a little kid, time itself changes properties; it now speeds up and slows down in unpredictable ways. When you're trying to get somewhere, it whizzes past; yet during those interminable eons when you're waiting with your child for poop to come, time and all biological processes have been known to come to an actual halt.

I'm not sure which part of the child-owning process causes this—whether childbirth itself causes a hormonal aberration that screws up a person's internal clock, or if it's simply that little children are maniacal when it comes to thinking up new ways to make you late, or to bore you. But *something* happens to change your getting-places timetable.

No matter how organized you used to be, now just getting you and one tiny child to the park takes as much effort as it once would have taken you to get an entire crew of people to Mount Everest.

A simple trip to the store

Let's look at a simple trip to the store. You perhaps foolishly decide one morning that you and your child can do a productive thing together, which would be to pick up some milk, eggs, bread, and one other item which you wish you could remember, but you can't because you made the list the night before, after midnight.

Here are the steps that have to happen before that simple trip to the store can take place:

You tell your child—we'll call him Daniel—that you need to go to the store, and he needs to stop playing now and change his clothes. For the record, Daniel is wearing your plastic rain hat, a green feather boa from the dress-up box, and one Clifford the Red Dog slipper on his hand.

Daniel says he doesn't want to go to the store.

You say it will be fun. First, you say, we'll find you some clothes and get dressed.

Daniel says he'll wear the boa.

You say blue corduroy pants, and you go to find them.

Boa!

Pants.

Boa! Boa! Boa! Boa! Boa!

Not in public. The boa is just for home.

Boa! Boa! BOA!

You find the pants under his bed and go off to find Daniel again. He's hiding behind the couch. You crouch down and try to grab his foot. He runs away. Laughing, trying to pretend this is a fun game, you chase him.

You catch him after only two times around the living room–dining room–kitchen circuit and realize you forgot to bring his underwear with you. Dragging him by the arm while he giggles and tries to squirm away, you make your way back to his dresser drawer and get underwear.

The phone rings. Daniel sprints off in the direction of the garage.

It's a telemarketer, curious as to whether you're truly happy with your long distance telephone service. You hang up and find Daniel in the garage, sitting behind the furnace.

I'll race you upstairs, you say, and after three minutes of picking at a scab on his knee, he agrees to this and you let him outrun you to the living room. He hides behind the couch once again, laughing. You drag him out. Less laughter than before.

Sitting on him, you manage to get him installed in the underwear and blue corduroy pants while he playfully kicks your kidneys.

The phone rings again. It's your mother, asking if you happen to remember where it was that Aunt Gladys and Uncle Robert went on vacation in 1974—that place they raved about. Was it St. Thomas or Thomasville? You have no idea. She says you sound snippy. You say you're tired, busy, exasperated, sleep deprived, and all you want is to go to the store.

Oh, she says. Well, I remember when *you* were that age, and—

Ma, you say, I have to go. I'll think about the Aunt Gladys question.

Daniel prances around the room in his corduroy pants and the boa.

You say, Now let's get you a shirt.

Daniel says he has to go to the bathroom, so you hurriedly take off the corduroy pants and the underwear and race him to the potty chair since this going to the bathroom thing hasn't been working out so well lately.

He sits on the potty chair for seven and a half minutes, waiting for pee to come. Every time you try to leave the room, he stands up and works on peeling a little patch of wallpaper in the bathroom, so you sit there and watch him, periodically saying, "Is the pee coming yet?" He's not sure.

The phone rings. It's a telemarketer wondering if you'd like some aluminum siding. You wouldn't.

Daniel yells that the boa got wet in the potty.

You say, How did that happen? And then realize you don't want to know. In fact, you would hate to know. You say it's okay because the boa isn't going to the store anyway, since Daniel is going to wear a shirt. You go off to find his sweatshirt.

When you come back, you see Daniel has green feathers in his mouth.

Were you eating the boa? The boa that you just peed on?

No.

Then how did the boa feathers get in your mouth?

He does a little dance to illustrate that he doesn't know.

You put the boa up on the closet shelf—he screams—and you somehow, in a record-breaking two minutes, manage to put his sweatshirt on him.

I hungry, he says.

You say, Let's get a snack to take with us to the store.

Ice cream!

Not ice cream in the car.

Popsicles!

No. Something dry. Maybe a cracker.

Feathers!

No. We don't eat feathers.

I eat feathers.

That wasn't good. You shouldn't eat that boa. It's yucky.

Let's fix crackers and cheese.

So you go to the kitchen and fix crackers and cheese—five pairs of them. The phone rings, but you let it ring. After a while, it stops. You put the crackers and cheese in a baggie.

When you turn around Daniel is wearing his Clifford slippers. He says, Man want to talk to Daddy.

Who?

I don't know.

Did you answer the phone?

Yes. Man says Daddy to call him.

Who was it?

I don't know. He tell me his number. But I can't write!

He laughs uproariously.

Was he somebody from work? Was he Mr. Green?

Daniel laughs and prances off. I ready to go!

You have to wear regular shoes. Where are your socks?

No socks! Clifford!

Can't wear Clifford slippers outside. Let's look for your socks.

One sock is in the drawer—miracle!—but then you remember that the other one is on the floor beside the dryer. You go to get it.

When you get back, Daniel is working on unzipping his corduroy pants. He says the pee came while you were gone.

You take off wet corduroy pants, wet underwear, and take him to the bedroom and close the door—you *cannot* retrieve him from behind the couch one more time in this calendar year without going crazy!—and then you get a new pair of underwear and his Pokémon sweatpants.

You sit on him once again and put him in the new dry clothes, and while you're there you twist the socks onto his feet.

No socks! Cliffords!

Yes, socks.

Cliffords!

Listen to me. You *have* to wear your shoes and socks.

Injured silence. Then: Bell grow shoes.

You work on forcing the feet into the socks and say nothing.

Bell grow shoes! Bell grow shoes! Bell grow shoes! Bell grow shoes!

Bells don't grow shoes, you say. (Yet another statement that, until now, has never been uttered in the history of the world.)

BELL GROW SHOES!

You go to the closet and stare at the floor. Red plastic boots? Sneakers? Your head is throbbing. You pick up the sneakers and take them to Daniel.

Yay! Bell grow shoes.

Ah, you think, Velcro shoes. You put his feet into the shoes, and even though he's trying to be cooperative, he still does that arching thing that makes his feet form into an almost perfect circle while you're trying to load them into the shoe. But at last you get them in, fasten the Velcro, and head for the kitchen to get the crackers and cheese snack.

You look for the list you made last night and then decide to go without it because from the bedroom you hear the ripping sound of Velcro detaching.

Daniel, leave your shoes on! you yell.

Me like bell grow.

I know, but leave them on.

You get snack together, find your purse (for some reason it's in the sink—you'll try to figure out why later), get your sweater and Daniel's sweater, and go to find him.

He's wearing one shoe.

You look for the other one and finally find it in the couch cushions. While you search for it, begging him to tell you where it is, he walks around in circles saying, "Uh-oh, uh-oh." You think later today you might have to call in some mental health professionals.

Finally you get everything together next to the front door, take Daniel by the hand and lead him to the car, put him into the car seat even though he's arching his back, buckle him in, get your keys, start the engine, drive to the store.

When you get there, thirteen minutes later, you get out, unbuckle Daniel's car seat. That's when you notice there's cheese smeared all over the seat belt and Daniel's wearing no shoes at all.

Where are they? you say.

He smiles at you. Cheese good!

Where are your shoes? On the floor? Under the car seat? What did you do with them?

Out the window, he says. I throwed them out the window.

You realize you don't need milk and bread so very badly after all—and besides, when you look down, you see that you're still wearing your bedroom slippers yourself.

You drive back home, stopping to pick up Velcro sneakers in the middle of the road two blocks from your house.

When you walk in the front door, the phone is ringing. It's your mother. St. Thomas, she says. It was St. Thomas where they went on that great vacation.

Clothes make the man

Just when it seems you're getting this parenthood thing down and can manage to look in the mirror each morning without thinking you look like you've been hit by a truck, along comes yet another blow delivered by your child: you dress weird. You don't look good most of the time. And everyone knows it.

God knows why this gets to you. You're looking at some-one, after all, whose best idea of high fashion is plastering her face with stickers.

I was found to be abusing my fashion responsibilities nearly every day. My plaid wool pants were deemed yucky. My boots were ugly. My bedroom slippers had lost most of their fuzziness and didn't even have a cartoon character on them. Why didn't I wear red lipstick like the nursery school teacher did? Couldn't my hair just be hanging into my face so I could toss it back and forth? It was a little like living with my mother again.

Once I was walking downtown with my three-and-a-half-year-old son, and he stopped at the window of a formal wear shop and stared at the bright, sequined numbers dis-played in the windows, dresses so slinky and brightly colored that it hurt your eyes to look at them for more than a few seconds.

"I just wish you would wear that every day," he said with a sigh. "But I know you won't."

My daughters were even more despairing of my fashion sense. The jeans and sweatshirts I lived in caused them to shake their heads in disappointment. "You are a grown-up and you could wear anything you want," said my daughter one time, "and I do not see why you won't even wear a crown!"

They also thought it was pathetic that I had a closet filled with high-heeled shoes—left over from a previous in-carnation when I worked in an office where everyone dressed up—and yet day after day I wore sneakers.

"When you were a bride, did you wear your veil every day for years?" one of them wanted to know.

"No, just for the ceremony," I said.

"Of *course*," she said, as though this is exactly what she would expect from someone with so little imagination. "Don't you think Daddy would have thought you were pretty if you wore it every night at dinner? You could have it instead of your napkin if you spilled anything."

Meanwhile, I noticed that items of my clothing kept disappearing into the children's rooms. The high heels, of course, had to be confiscated so they could be put to good use; but along with those went my summer nightgown (later I saw it had become a bridal veil); the satin purse I had once taken to a formal dance; and a black strapless bra, which for a while served as a bed for a couple of Beanie Babies but then assumed its rightful position as a piece of risqué underwear, stuffed with tennis balls when it was being worn by my child. Belts, scarves, hats, long skirts—all my old clothing slowly made their way downstairs into the dress-up box, where it became part of my kids' daily outfits.

It was when my three-year-old insisted on wearing a purple taffeta bridesmaid's dress to nursery school that I drew the line.

"You have to quit taking all my stuff—and no, you can't wear this to school! It drags on the floor, you'll get paint and markers on it—and besides that, it's a hideous shade of purple!"

She gave me a level look and put her hands on her hips. "*Someone* has to make sure this dress gets seen by other people, and I can see that *you* won't do it."

Helpful fashion advice for adults from
the world of preschoolers

- Wear Winnie-the-Pooh clothing as often as possible.
- Bunny slippers go with everything.
- Your lipstick should always match your shirt.
- Everyone respects you more when you wear glitter.
- For special occasions, kitty whiskers tastefully drawn on your cheeks add a whimsical touch.
- Spandex is so nice in the office.
- Always wear high heels, even with socks.

New fashion trends you didn't think of

The most important factor in little kids' clothing decisions is that each one must support one's independence. Forget what the fashion moguls are calling for—sometimes clothing, like the creative use of the potty, is the only way you can stand up and scream, "I'm *me*, not you!"

My friend Helena was doing the family laundry one morning when her three-year-old daughter, Janie, said suddenly, "I don't want you to wash my clothes. I'm going to wear dirty clothes now."

Helena had been willing to go along with the raccoon skin cap, the ballerina skirt worn on the head as an elaborate veil, and the torn-up fuzzy bathrobe being worn for trips in the car, but there was no way she could go along with dirty clothes.

"Janie," she said, "I have to wash your clothes. You can't wear dirty ones."

"But I'm going to! I'm only wearing dirty clothes!" Janie jumped into the pile of dirty clothes and tried to carry off her own clothes.

"No, Janie."

"Yes!"

"No! Don't wash those clothes, Mommy!"

Helena started the washing machine anyway, and Janie fell to the floor, screaming and frothing at the mouth. It was about a Stage Three tantrum—there were flecks of spittle flying everywhere, and ear protection was possibly needed, but helmets weren't yet required. Helena stepped over Janie, carefully leaping so she wouldn't be bitten as she passed over.

Janie lay there, calling on the forces of death and darkness to overtake Helena, but finally got up, stomped into her bedroom, and got all her clean underwear out of the drawer and took them outside to the patio. There she rubbed them into the dirt and mud, and then took off all her regular clothes and put on the muddy underwear.

Helena could hear her through the window: "I will *not* wear clean clothes! I am *never* wearing clean clothes again, and she can't make me! She thinks she's the boss of me, but she has *never* been the boss of me. That is over, over, over. I am *not* a baby anymore, and I always hated her. I will tell Daddy about this, and then we will run away and nobody will ever speak to her again. Even Grandma will come with us when she finds out where we are! I hate her! I hate her and her stupid ideas about clean clothes!"

Helena listened, wondering at which point she might have to call in the psychiatrists and social workers, but she kept doing the laundry, and Janie played in the sandbox right outside the screen door. And then she came in for lunch, said she wanted to put on some different clothes.

"My underwear got all dirty outside," she said.

Helena said it certainly had. And neither one of them ever brought the matter up again. Later Janie decided she was going to wear some cut-off sleeves of an old gray T-shirt as a headband and a necklace made from a huge rubber band and the magnetic letters off the refrigerator. For three days, she wore those, along with one red rain boot and one Mary Jane patent leather shoe.

But hey, at least everything was clean.

Regular household chores in only twice the time

My friend Angela says one of the best things about having little children around is that they are so willing to help out with the household chores. They're not jaded, she says, like older kids who roll their eyes at you if you so much as suggest they scoot their feet over so you can vacuum underneath them.

Angela does not have any children. I think she got her information from the fact that once she heard a little kid say to his mother, "I wash the floor myself! Me do it!"

The thing about child labor is that it is never worth it. Never. A child who is willing to wash the floor really means that he is excited about the possibility of throwing water and soap on the ground and then sliding in it. In fact, I'm convinced that little children don't realize that cleaning has any purpose other than to amuse and add to the general havoc.

In fact, when a child offers to help you with anything, you need to realize she is speaking another language. Here's a helpful chart to show you what your child really means:

She says:	She means:
I wash the dishes for you.	Let's throw the dishes on the floor just to see what kind of noise they make.
I want to sweep the floor.	I want to knock over lamps with broom.
I clean the potty.	I'm in the mood for splashing in forbidden water.
I feed the kitty.	I'm starving for something crunchy.
I want to dust the tables.	Let's see if these vases could break the front window if we throw them hard.

People will tell you that it's important that you teach your child how to do housework; otherwise, they say, how will she ever know what to do once she gets her own apartment? Do not fall for this line. So few toddlers move out on their own that it's not worth worrying about. And even in the best-case scenario, you probably have about fifteen years before there's so much as a dormitory room looming on the horizon—and there has been no documented case of a teenager ever doing housework in a dormitory room. The fact is, you have eons of time before you need to bring up the skills of dishwashing and toilet cleaning. Surely, sometime after she's gotten over her fixation with smashing crockery and sliding in suds, you can find a good moment to demonstrate just how civilized humans do the dishes.

So instead of thinking up ways for your child to be helpful around the house, perhaps you would live longer and enjoy your life more if you simply used that energy trying to find ways of doing the housework without your child ever noticing. With some kids—the kind who are ever on the alert for more ways of wallowing in chaos—you may have to get very tricky indeed. My friend Marge, for instance, will only mop the floor during Barney marathons, when she's sure her kids won't budge. Ellen has been known to sneak out of bed in the middle of the night so she can clean the toilet without having powdered cleanser exploding all over the bathroom. And I went through years when I rushed home early from work so that I could sweep before they got home from day care. It's so much easier than arguing with them—or picking up the glass from broken lamps after they succeeded in helping me.

Once my friend Anna told me she'd had a close call with her mother-in-law, who had told the children about dusting.

"She described the whole process to them!" said Anna. "How a person could squirt stuff on the table and then wipe it around with a rag. I kept trying to get her attention so I could shush her, but she just kept going on and on and on. I don't think I'll ever have a moment's peace again."

"It's hard," I said, "when trust has been shattered that way. You'd think a mother-in-law would understand that there are some topics children shouldn't be exposed to. After all, she's had children herself."

"Well, I'll tell you one thing: she certainly never mentioned dusting to her son! Nope, I think this is just a case of her trying to get revenge on me for the fact that I forgot to send her the newborn pictures before I sent them to my own mother."

"Well, obviously you can't trust her around the children alone," I said. "Next she'll be spouting off about cleaning the oven."

The Arsenic Hour

I know this is not a very nice concept—that there is a whole chunk of the day named for rat poison—but soon after giving birth, you discover that for some reason babies think the period in the evening between, say, five and seven, is *the* saddest bit of time known to mankind, and they need to wail continuously about it. And this notion does not diminish when a person gets to the advanced age of, say, two or three. Even by the age of five, most of your small humans are running around being obnoxious and irritating at the very point in the day when you might like to kick back with a dry martini and a foot massage.

No one knows exactly why this is, or why it's so universal. Who told kids that evening was horrible, anyway? Where exactly are they getting this information? Without them around, it's actually a pretty pleasant time of day. A person gets to eat again, for instance—and that's always a positive thing. And it's getting dark outside, so you can come inside and think about how great it's going to be to go to sleep at some point.

I hardly think that kids are giving the five o'clock hour a fair trial. If they would just stop screaming and let us take a freaking breath so we can get dinner on the table, that would be a major improvement right there.

Instead, this is the hour they choose for the falling-down-on-the-floor, head-banging temper tantrums—and if they're too tired to muster the energy for that, then they're sure to be hanging underfoot, pondering the large, existential questions like "Who was I before I was born?" and "How many times have I ever sneezed?" (If you don't have accurate records documenting the number of sneezes, the correct number is 217, delivered in a voice of great confidence.)

People will give you all kinds of advice about how to survive the Arsenic Hour. I myself have written magazine articles on this topic, where I was supposed to give people tips on how to live through the dinner hour. I'm ashamed now to admit that I've perpetuated the idea that "tips" can get one through this, day after day. The tips that family experts mentioned to me were things like: Ask your child to wash the vegetables for you.

Now this is something that only someone who does not currently own a small child would think of—because any parent can see that it's not going to be helpful to the general horribleness of the Arsenic Hour to add potatoes and carrots being hurled in your direction, especially while your child is simultaneously pouring water across the kitchen floor. This is the kind of situation that can only send a person out shopping for a better brand of arsenic.

The other tips experts had for us included taking an Arsenic Hour time-out for yourself. You know, simply refuse to buy into the idea that dinner needs to get cooked and the children need you to count up their lifetime sneezes. They thought it would be helpful if you said something like, "Mommy is feeling a little bit cranky right now, so I'm going to take a hot bubble bath with the aromatherapy candles and the mellow flute tape. Naturally, I'm going to have to lock the bathroom door, so I need you to sit quietly until I get back, and then we'll have some Quality Time together."

This type of situation can only result in legal authorities having to come to your house to deal with the Arsenic Hour themselves. And believe me, they're not going to be any more cheerful about it than you are.

Nine consequences of picking up a magazine

- Your child will get thirsty.
- Your child will get hungry.
- The toilet will get stopped up by a wooden block that has been thrown there and has then expanded to double its normal size. (Eventually a plumber will have to replace the entire toilet, but you won't know that for a while.)
- A glass of orange juice will "leap off" the counter and land on the floor, where it breaks into an astonishing number of shards.
- You will need to make an emergency trip for Band-Aids.
- The wallpaper will start peeling off the wall in the back bedroom.
- Your child's bangs will end up two inches shorter.
- The Velcro on his sneakers will become exhausted and will never stick again.
- Your child will need to go to the bathroom forty-seven times in a row—the first documented case of a human getting corduroy burn from pulling pants up and down so many times in a row with no discernible waste products being eliminated.

The new definition of class

It used to be that class was defined as someone who could remain cool while she was waiting in a train station on a ninety-degree day, and then the train wasn't air-conditioned and she had to stand next to people who were perspiring, but because she had so much class, she didn't even appear to notice. She just smiled and looked beautiful. (I think it was Audrey Hepburn and Jackie Kennedy who were best at this kind of class.)

Once you have children, you don't think of class in the same way ever again. Class, as my friend Bert describes it, is when you can walk through an airport holding a child who is throwing up massive amounts of cheese Danish and orange juice—and then you take her into the men's room to clean her up, and businessmen rushing in slip in your child's vomit and fall down.

Now, this is where the classy part comes in, according to Bert. Throughout the whole ordeal, you keep your head down and you do not appear to notice the very maniacal stares people are giving you. You just keep mopping up surfaces with damp paper towels and reassuring your child that eventually she will run out of cheese Danish and orange juice, and that the two of you will get out of this airport, and yes, people will stop staring at the two of you. Of course, you don't believe a word you're saying, but don't let that stop you.

There are lots of other times when you get to be classy, too. In fact, early childhood is packed with these kinds of opportunities. This is one of the chief occupations of little kids, discovering new ways of testing your ability to wince and smile at the same time.

There will be lots of opportunities, believe me.

My friend Susan, who had been single for a while, was finally dating again once her child turned four. (Up until that age, she said, there was no point in trying to go out with a man, because she was so tired all she did was drop off to sleep during that time of the evening when a man was in the mood to tell his life story. After a year of no second dates, she packed it in for a long while.) But there she was, seeing someone great at last, and after the obligatory first four dates and the hearing of his life story and the telling of her life story, she at last invited him to her house for dinner and to meet Ryan.

Now, Ryan is one of the nicest kids you'd ever want to meet, and he really was excited about the idea of possibly getting a new man to entertain—so excited, in fact, that he kept bringing out objects to show the new guy. First there was the toilet brush, of course (you can't really know someone who hasn't seen and appreciated your various cleaning utensils), and then out came his collection of Beanie Babies and the stuffed bear he slept with since he was two weeks old (you have to make sure a new person won't laugh at something personal like that), but then, for the pièce de résistance, he brought out the bathroom trash can, where Susan had unfortunately disposed of a sanitary napkin.

Of course she could see what was about to happen, as Ryan lugged the trash can into the living room and started going through its contents. But she couldn't get there quite in time. First the empty toilet paper roll was put on display, as she was saying, "Now, Ryan, take that back—" and then, as she was sprinting across the room and ready to make a nose dive tackle, he pulled out the sanitary napkin and waved it around the room, saying, "Oh, no! Who got hurt? Who's hurt, Mom?"

Susan, by her own admission, was not able to muster true class in this situation. She screamed and grabbed for the thing, then ran with it and Ryan to the back of the house, where she told him he should never, ever in his whole life *look* at a trash can again, and never ever *ever* discuss its contents with anyone in the whole world. She was dangerously close, she says now, to making a rope from the sheets and simply climbing out the window with Ryan, and never returning to her apartment again.

The new guy, however—now, *that's* where the class came in—after a few minutes, softly knocked on the door, announced that dinner was done, and asked if he might once again see that wonderful toilet brush. For the rest of the evening, he let Ryan sit on his lap—and kept giving Susan comforting smiles and little winks.

Later, showing real class, he married her. Now, of course, *his* most private and personal possessions are being trotted out at dinner parties. But he can't say he wasn't warned.

The fork in your briefcase: how the people at work now see you

Once you have a child, it seems as though everyone else should have one, too. You're shocked, in fact, to realize that there are still people who show up for work without a disposable diaper sticking out of their pocket and with no jelly stains on their shoulders. They seem somehow sadly underdressed. Also, when one has to do with them—say, in the workplace cafeteria, or washing up in the restroom—their conversations revolve around such inane things as good restaurants they've been to lately. With only the mildest encouragement, they'll tell you about wines they've tasted, newly invented vegetables that are now known to contain the most delicious antioxidants ever, and how many waiters it took to serve their ten-course, low-calorie meal last weekend.

Sometimes they'll politely inquire if *you've* had any memorable dining out experiences recently. It's best if you can hold off telling the true account of your trip to Chuck E.

Cheese. People without kids won't understand that a person really can have actual fun standing in the middle of a room filled with 157 toddlers, all of whom are hurling plastic balls at one another, dangling from a climbing/sliding board/ski-jump apparatus, and, of course, shrieking. They won't even appreciate your rendition of the dancing bears who come out on the stage specifically to sing sappy songs about birthdays, but, just the same, manage to terrify nearly everyone in the place. And you'll not get laughs from childless people, even when you describe how your keys got thrown out by the waiter, and that you had to wade through two Dumpsters filled with orange soda and discarded pizza crusts while your kid climbed on you and smeared tomato paste and Parmesan cheese into your scalp.

I have tried to talk to childless people before, trying to achieve some understanding, but believe me, telling them of these deeply hilarious and personal disasters is only a mistake. They will feel sorry for you and your miserable adventures, and although they may snicker politely, they're really horrified. Then, when you attend the next staff meeting and pull a fork instead of a ballpoint pen out of your briefcase, they'll be shaking their heads in pity and whispering to one another that it's only a matter of time before you're completely off the deep end. And from then on, everything flaky you do—losing your keys, forgetting your password, running out of work one day screaming about children shoving nickels in their nostrils—will be chalked up to your status as a wretched, freaked-out parent, obviously unable to run your life properly.

Best if you can keep your descriptions to a minimum, except, of course, when you are talking to other people who know what it's like. You might sum up your evening at Chuck E. Cheese, for instance, by saying, "Oh, we had a delightful family dinner at a very *interactive* restaurant that specializes in cheese concoctions and features an exotic floor show. Later, I got some aerobic exercise and did some weight lifting outside, while having a scalp massage using organic vegetable and dairy products—those of the highest antioxidant content, of course."

When you've made it sound so good that they want to go there themselves, you know you've made parenthood look good.

Things you never thought you'd say but now say all the time

- No, you can't wash your pillow in the bathtub.
- Stop rubbing up against parked cars.
- Peas aren't to be eaten with a knife.
- Take that peanut butter out of the CD slot.
- Don't wipe your nose on the drapes.
- Stop jumping on the couch with the dog's leash in your mouth.
- You can't wear a whole roll of toilet paper to nursery school.
- If you put that dime in your nose one more time, you're going to lose it.
- Stop running on the dining room table! Always walk when you're up that high!
- How much is a good straitjacket in my size?

The telephone—why it's never your turn to talk

You knew, going into parenthood, that there would of course come a time when the telephone was absolutely unavailable to the adults of the household. You just probably thought it would be during, say, the adolescent years, when humans experience a biological need to have conversations that consist of someone saying, "I mean, he was like, and then I was like, and then she was like, and then we were all like . . ." for upward of eight hours at a time.

But no. The telephone actually becomes an instrument of desirability very early in life, much earlier than most social scientists have been documenting. Just as soon as a kid realizes the magic of the phone—that it's something you often love so much you caress it to your face and say words to it—well, they've just got to have it, too. During babyhood, it sometimes works to provide them with their own little toy rendition of a telephone, but by the time they're three, they see this as the hoax that it is. And by the time they're five, they're so much more advanced than you when it comes to telephone technology that they're E-mailing you at work to ask if they can have their very own fax machines and Internet connections with their telephones.

In the meantime, though, they always seem to have possession of the phone. Or at least they seem to monitor its usage and its location in the house. When we were toddlers, intent on dismantling our parents' lives, one thing we really could never control was the telephone. It stayed basically in one place, attached to the wall—and quite often, it was up too high and was too heavy for us to have much chance of wrecking it. But now with phones weighing about three ounces and lying about in all kinds of places—including purses—it's no longer off their minds for very long.

The fact is, children see early on which is the good stuff in the house, and which equipment might be considered boring and useless. The phone, the remote control device, the mop, your lipstick, and the stereo system are all highly desirable, of course. There's not too much in the category of too-boring-even-for-a-cursory-dismantling, but toy telephones are definitely considered contemptible by any child over the age of six months.

Worse than their fascination with playing with the phone

when nobody else is using it is their insistence on being the Main Phone Answerer. Many toddlers think all they have to do is just hold it in their hands, and the phone itself will do all the work. They outrun you to pick it up once it rings, and then stand there, silently holding it, while you can hear through the earpiece, "Hello? Hello? *Hello?*"

So you say, "Say hello, darling. Say hello into the phone."

The child does his best impression of a Heavy Breather.

"Say hello!"

The child now sounds like Darth Vader and is looking at you murderously. You can see his knuckles gripping the receiver are white.

"Come on, honey, just say hello—"

Darth Vader after a three-mile run.

"Honey, why don't you hand the phone to Mommy? Come on, sweetie, you can talk on it later."

"I talk now," he says. Then silence.

"Say hello," you coax. "Come on, just say hello."

But he's frozen into place.

The person on the other end is now desperately trying to plead with *you.* "Take the phone! For God's sake, take the phone away from him! I need to tell you something!"

Just as you're ready to make your move and tackle your child, grabbing the phone out of his hands, he springs into action, shouts, "Hello! Good-bye!" and then slams the phone down.

You look at each other.

He says, "I talk on phone."

It rings again, and you realize you have the beginnings of a long-term headache.

4

New Things to Worry About in the Middle of the Night

You are worried. Of course you're worried. You'd be a fool not to notice that the world is an unstable place for little people—that even for big people it's not great all the time. Sometimes you can't fall asleep at night for worrying about things like: is the wind blowing so hard it's going to knock down some trees, which will fall precisely on the kid's bed? Are the spiders behind the toilet the infamous brown recluse spiders, and do you need to get up right now and go and extinguish them once and for all? Is he always going to say "lellow" for yellow, and if so, will people make fun of him his whole life, or will they find it as charming as you do?

Here's an incomplete list of all the things you will think of at one time or another, things you probably can't prevent anyway, but somehow it feels necessary to worry about them just the same:

- A pebble will get stuck in the lawn mower and come flinging out and catch your kid in the eye
- Bacterial meningitis
- Ticks
- You'll take her to the ballet in New York City, and

a piece of a building will fall off the thirty-fourth floor right as you are walking beneath it on the sidewalk and kill you both. And this is before you even get to the ballet.

- Big scary dogs not on leashes
- You will forget to cut the peanut-butter-and-marmalade sandwich into precise isosceles triangles, and your child will eat no food at nursery school for the whole day.
- Pedophiles in the park
- Electric outlets at other people's houses
- Your car is going to get so cluttered with paper cups, broken toys, fast-food wrappers, and unidentifiable food substances that, should you ever get pulled over by a cop, he'll be legally required to have it condemned by the Health Department.
- You'll be in a bad mood the day he asks, "Why was I born?"
- Your child will be told by someone else that the stuff on TV commercials really *is* for sale.
- Bullies on the playground
- What if it's *your* kid who turns out to be the bully on the playground?
- One day you won't be able to open the childproof lid, and your child will have to help you.
- Men will never again smile and wave at you in the car, now that you're the driver of a minivan.
- Evil
- You shouldn't have put 911 on speed dial.
- Guns, supposedly locked, at friends' houses
- She's never going to recover emotionally from the death of the goldfish, and especially the moment when she sees you flush it down the toilet.
- Your child will sing "Ninety-nine Bottles of Beer on the Wall" and "What Shall We Do with the

Drunken Sailor?" at school and will explain that this is how you've sung him to sleep for the past three years.

- Your new lace teddy will be the featured item at show-and-tell.
- How are you going to ever help him study for the test of the state capitals when you can't for the life of you ever remember the capital of South Dakota?
- Someone will tell him about AIDS in fifth grade, and he'll never get married.
- You are hopelessly stuck with the ten pounds left over from pregnancy, and now they have added their own ten pounds.
- You're not flossing his teeth correctly.
- She'll grow up and marry somebody you hate but you'll try your best to mask your true feelings, but the one time you say, "Well, dear, he *seems* to be trying harder," she'll get so mad at you that she'll never speak to you again, and you won't ever see your grandchildren.
- He will decide to cook by himself when you're asleep.
- You will always be having conversations about poop at the dinner table.

5

Life Is Nothing But a Big Fat Holiday

Happy birthday presents to me...

By the time the average American human is three years old, he is completely enthralled with the idea that a day comes around every now and then that is just for him. What a concept! A whole day when people are forced—*forced!*—to come and sing him a song, bring him wrapped presents, and do whatever he tells them to do. They can't take the presents back home, either. Plus, there's the blowing out the candles, which is when a child is legally permitted to spit all over an entire chocolate cake, and nobody even yells.

For months leading up to the birthday, little else gets discussed. Who will be allowed to come? Not David, after the way he didn't share his rubber band one day last November. Probably not Cody, the way she wouldn't get off the swing when your child wanted it—and then when she finally did give the swing up because the teacher made her, then Roddy got on it—so Roddy probably can't be invited either.

This may be when you gently point out that without David, Cody, and Roddy, how much of a fun party is this going to be?

"Those are your best friends from school," you say.

"Don't you want your friends to come be with you on your birthday?"

"Weellll . . . what presents will they bring me?"

You try to explain that it doesn't work that way in the world, that we want our friends to celebrate with us, presents or no presents—but your child has already figured the Present System out for himself, and he wants the loot, thank you very much. Still, after weeks of juggling the guest list around—Cody keeps getting dropped and reinstated several times a day—everyone is invited, and before you know it, it's time to spit on the cake and open the presents.

An hour before the guests are set to arrive, you realize with horror that your kid is more high-strung than he's ever been in his life. He even cried when the oven-timer went off. He screamed that he hated you when you asked him if he'd had any breakfast. And he fell on the floor in a purple rage when the doorbell rang and it was only somebody wanting to mow the lawn, not the mailman bringing yet more presents.

He's so out of control that you're considering dosing him with Benadryl and then, once he's out cold, having him lie in state on the couch for the duration of the party. But no doubt, on a day like this, the Benadryl would have the opposite effect, and instead of sleeping, he'd be hysterically running around the room, eating the party decorations, and punching out the elderly relatives. By the time the lighting of the candles came, he'd be setting fire to the curtains.

Since it would be tacky of you to run away, the only alternative may be having a little Birthday Party Rehearsal.

You sit down and calmly tell him what's going to happen—guests will arrive one by one, and he will stand with you and tell them all hello, and very politely take their presents and stack them in a pile, and—

"And then I open them!"

"Well, not yet. First we put them in a pile until everyone is there—"

"I open them!"

"Yes, yes, you will open them. But we'll tell everybody hello, and then we'll play a game together . . ."

"A game of open presents!"

"Now, when you're opening the presents, what do you say if someone gives you something you don't like?"

"I say 'Yuck!' "

"Oh, dear. Let's talk about this. If you say 'yuck,' how will that make the person feel?"

"That they shouldn't bring a yucky present next time."

"No, no. I think it would be better to say, 'Thank you for the nice present.' "

"But you said I *didn't* like it."

"You might not like it, but you can't hurt people's feelings. They bought it for you because they thought you would like it. So you need to thank them."

"Okay. I say, 'Thank you, this is yuck.' "

"Just 'thank you.' Can you do that? Can you say 'thank you'?"

"No."

"Let's practice. Let's say you're opening a present, and inside it's—white socks! What do you say?"

"I hate socks. I don't want socks."

"I know. That's why we're practicing. In case someone gives you socks, and you don't want to hurt their feelings—"

"Is somebody going to give me socks? Did you tell people I wanted socks?"

"No, no, I didn't. But someone might just give you socks anyway. They might think that's a good present."

"Socks can't be a good present! Nobody wants socks for their birthday! Who told them that?"

"It just might happen. Sometimes we get things that

aren't our very favorite things, and we still want to be nice about it. We don't want to hurt people's feelings."

Your child looks at you suspiciously. "I thought this was going to be good day for me."

"It will be a good day for you. It's your birthday. You just need to be nice to people, that's all."

There's a sputtering silence. Then he says, "I don't think it's a good day if you have to be nice the *whole* time!"

By the time the first guest arrives, he's ready to clobber her. "Is this socks?" he says, when she hands him her present. "Because you might as well just take it back. I can't say 'thank you' for socks!"

... and okay, happy birthday presents to you, too

Things get even more delicate when the birthday is someone else's—and you and your child are the ones bringing a present. Let me tell you right off that it's best if you can find a reason to leave the party as soon as possible. Drop your child off and then start a bout of fake coughs if you have to, in order to be excused. But get out of there as soon as you can. No three- or four-year-old is at his best when he's having to hand over some beautifully wrapped present to another kid. As far as he's concerned, that gift is on loan only, and he'll be not only playing with it during the party but will most likely want to leave with it as well.

This is a rule of birthday parties. There are always a few kids who don't think gift giving is an appropriate activity—and besides that, they'd like the Happy Birthday Song to have their own names inserted in there, too. All too often, the birthday child has to come over and deck a few of his friends, just to establish whose party this is anyway.

This will lead to a scrimmage, a couple of tantrums (often the Stage Four variety, with help from outsiders), and at least three kids crying. I've been to birthday parties when the entire contingent of guests was in tears, and the mothers hovering over the whole mess only made it worse. If the hostess is not careful, everyone will be crying, adults and children alike.

There are other rules for birthday parties, too—some that you may not have realized. Here they are, so you won't be surprised:

The Birthday Party Rules for Preschoolers

- Someone, and perhaps everyone, has to cry.
- At least one kid is allergic to the ingredients in the cake.
- Someone always flushes something unfortunate in the potty: party favors, rolls of paper towels, the present they brought.
- Someone's shoe gets hopelessly lost—is that also in the potty?
- One kid always throws up, often at the table.
- Your child has to be sent to her room at least twice.
- You need a stiff drink and fifteen hours of sleep to recover—if recovery is even possible, which you doubt.

Mother's Day

Mother's Day is definitely in the Hit Parade of kids' favorite holidays, possibly because nursery school teachers push it so strenuously. Up until now, you may have been seeing Mother's Day from a daughter's perspective only, which translates to: Oh, my God, why can't I remember to buy and mail the card on time even *once*?

But now that you're the mom of a kid who knows how to write on paper plates or affix painted macaroni to a jar, you're going to be seeing Mother's Day in a whole new light. It's one of your main present-gathering holidays of the year.

I have Mother's Day presents that I still am responsible for producing at a moment's notice, years later. I have a paper plate, for instance, with two portraits of myself, drawn by my four-year-old. One says Mommy Young and the other says Mommy Old. In the first I'm wearing an orange miniskirt (I have never worn an orange miniskirt) and a green shirt, and in the other I'm wearing the same thing but holding a bag and a cane.

I also have a paper plate—paper plates are the true medium for Mother's Day presents, in nursery school teachers' minds, apparently—that says "I love Mommy because she lets me go bowling with Daddy. We have fun." And of course there are the various aforementioned jars with elbow macaroni stuck to them. I am required even so many years later to keep my pencils in these—and to reglue any stray macaroni that insists on falling whenever the front door slams or someone steps too hard on the wood floors.

It can be a full-time job, keeping a Mother's Day present going. But nothing makes a kid as happy as discovering that he made something that you actually use.

The toughest Mother's Day challenge came home with my son when he was in kindergarten: an ivy leaf stuck in a bit of potting soil in a paper cup. This one leaf had received so much hugging and kissing that it was worn out from affection. My job, of course, was to keep it alive.

I managed to persuade the gift giver that hugging and kissing weren't as good for plants as they are for people, and together we repotted it into bigger and bigger pots over the years. It grew long tendrils, spiraling up toward the light wherever it could. It looped over vases and picture frames, drapery rods and lampshades in its quest to take over the world. We offered cuttings to everyone who visited our house; then we resorted to forcing people to take pieces of it home with them. For years, we gave cuttings as hostess gifts and birthday presents. For a while, I think, some people stopped coming to visit us because of our ivy plant.

At last it was so big that the roots could scarcely support it. It started to turn yellow and brown and get big spots on the leaves. One summer, when my kid was away at summer camp, I reluctantly moved it to the basement, where it could rest in the darkness, and, I hoped, shuffle off this mortal coil and find peace.

Instead, my son found it within five minutes after returning home from summer camp. "How could you kill off this plant?" he said. "I gave it to you for *Mother's Day*! Don't you remember?"

I was horribly guilty, but I explained that all things come to an end eventually—and this plant, lovely though it was, had had a longer run than most. "Look at it," I said. "It's clearly at death's door. Let it go in peace."

But naturally that was not to be. Our friends and neighbors were only too happy to bring us back the offspring of clippings we'd made them take over the years.

"I don't know if she'll be able to keep it alive," I heard my son tell one friend. "She has no respect for Mother's Day presents."

The Halloween negotiations

When you're three years old, hardly anything—even a birthday—is more incredible than the fact of Halloween.

You can see a three-year-old's eyes widen as the concept gets explained: We're going to dress you up in crazy clothes, then go outside *at night,* walk up to every house in the neighborhood, yell "Trick or treat!" and then the people have to give you *candy.*

Unfortunately, when you're three, you might not be able to appreciate this event to its fullest extent because—well, because you're still afraid of everything. For some, it can be horrifying to have to go out on the street where there are actual card-carrying clowns walking around, never mind the witches, ghosts, and human computer chips you see these days. And how to cope with all that sanctioned screaming other kids are doing at each door—it's truly mystifying that this is being allowed. And besides that, it's *dark* outside, and everybody is acting as if walking around out there is totally normal.

The year our daughter was three, she was so afraid of everything that I figured we'd be done with the whole trick-or-treat business in about six minutes flat. Then we'd come back home, put her to bed, and I'd eat the Milky Way bar the neighbors were sure to have given us—because what three-year-old cares about Milky Way bars?

I had it wrong. In spite of the fact that at home she refused to go into any room that was lit with anything less than a seventy-five-watt bulb on the grounds that monsters could be hiding out in the shadows, she charged up on porches where there were actual Authentic Witches stirring big steaming pots of witches' brew and threatening children.

"You can skip this house, if you want to," I told her. We both watched as a witch cackled at some kids and a ghost jumped out of a nest of spiderwebs on the porch.

"No, I think you get the best candy at a place like this," she whispered back.

It was this candy-at-any-cost attitude that landed us at

home two hours later with a haul that guaranteed a lifetime of hyperactivity and dextrose overload. And she wanted all of it for herself.

There is nothing like negotiating candy consumption with an irrational three-year-old to make you feel hideous about yourself. It is a battle of the wits in which you realize you have no weapons.

There the two of you are standing, in front of a pillow-case filled with 900,000 pieces of chocolate, and you are saying, "Okay, you can have one piece tonight, and one piece tomorrow." By your own calculations, you see that at that rate this candy will last until your child is ready for retirement. Anyone can see how ridiculous this idea is. In fact, your child doesn't even bother to take that news in. Instantly, she's plopped herself down in the middle of all the packages and, with computer speed and accuracy, sorted them into piles, memorized how many she has of each type, negotiated to eat five additional pieces that very minute— and, you suspect, quite possibly has devoured up to ten more pieces surreptitiously.

And the five pieces you let her have? One turns out to be a bag of M&Ms; another a package of Necco wafers with at least thirty-five pieces of candy in it; then a bag of candy corn; a full-size candy bar (*your* Milky Way, incidentally); and a package of Life Savers. All in all, you figure, she's had enough candy to fill Yankee Stadium.

And here's the worst part: When you asked her for *one piece*, she studied the pile for a long time before awarding you one Raisinette. Somehow, even by three, they know that Raisinettes are health foods, by Halloween standards.

Five zoomed-out hours later, as you're blearily tucking her into bed, she smiles up at you and says, "Tomorrow I eat the rest of the candy, and then let's go say 'Trick or treat' and get more."

Scaring Santa Claus

I have always had mixed feelings about the Santa Claus business—for all the usual reasons: guilt over telling a child a story so wild that you'll later have to untell it; middle-class anxiety over perpetuating the crassly commercial aspect of Christmas; and, of course, the dread of having to stand in long lines of screaming children so my child could have a moment with the Great Man Himself. I even thought briefly that we should be Santa Claus holdouts: perhaps my husband and I would simply tell our kids the day they were born that the whole business was just a myth, and be done with it. Then we could sleep late every Christmas.

I hadn't figured, though, on the way that *everyone* tells a little kid to be good because Santa Claus is coming. And even though we did mention to the kids in the delivery room that there was no Santa Claus, they forgot it nearly immediately. So before I could really plan out my Santa Claus strategy, what with being sleep deprived and all, I had a three-year-old neurotically planning her visit to the mall and worrying that maybe she hadn't been good enough for him to bring her presents. Of *course* she hadn't been good enough; we were coming off a six-month period where she'd had five or six tantrums a day, had cut the neighbors' hose with the scissors, and chewed the heads off her cousin's Barbies. She'd been so rotten I had started reading a book on how to recognize the signs of childhood schizophrenia.

"Tell me the questions he will ask me," she said. Then, in a worried voice: "Does he know about the hose?"

"No."

"But the song says he sees you when you're sleeping and when you're awake. He see'd me cut the hose."

"I don't think he's looking for that kind of thing."

"Well, what about the Barbies? I chewed their heads."

"But you were sorry. You said you wouldn't do it again."

"Sometimes I scream."

"Yes, you do scream."

"Does that make Santa Claus mad?"

I wanted to say that it makes Santa Claus so mad that she must never ever do it again, or risk not getting any presents whatsoever. But it's no good, perpetuating that view of Santa Claus as Interrogator and Judge of Toddlers. Besides, she'd just go into a complete meltdown of angst, and I'd spend the rest of my life trying to help her figure a way for her to make amends with Santa Claus. She'd probably just have more tantrums and eat more Barbie heads in her anxiety.

Even without the anxiety of having to make amends to Santa Claus, life was bad enough over the next few days. Riding in the car, she started a constant patter of Santa Claus talk: "I love Santa Claus so much. When I was little, I just liked him. But now I really love him. He is such a nice man to little children. Children are little, so he brings them lots of presents, anything they ask for. He sees how much they try, and he wants to do nice things for them. I might love him more than any other kid loves him." Then she leaned over, and whispered, "Do you think he hears me right now?"

One night she got up in the middle of the night. "I've got a great idea," she whispered at my bedside. She was whispering, of course, so she wouldn't disturb my sleep while she was waking me up. "When I go to see Santa Claus, I'll tell him about all the *good* things I did. Then, even if he knows the bad things, maybe the good things will be more."

I said wearily, "I really don't think Santa Claus cares about that."

"But the song says he does!"

"It's just a silly song. It's not real."

A few days later we ran into an off-duty Santa Claus lined up to get on a bus. I braced myself for the questions about why he has to take city buses if he has that wonderful sleigh and all the reindeer. Instead, she ran over to him and shouted, "I shared a cookie today at day care!"

He gave her a quizzical look, as if he'd quite forgotten that he was wearing a Santa Claus suit and so was supposed to be the keeper of little children's list of good deeds. Then he waved. "Okay! I'll remember!"

All the way home she worried over this. "I think he should have writed it down," she said. "I should have said my name. Let's go back and tell him I'm Stephanie. The day-care teacher says I look like a little girl who lives near her. He might think I'm a different girl."

"Santa Claus knows you," I said. "He's going to bring you presents."

When the time finally came to talk to him, she was eerily calm. We stood in line while she unloaded on me all her last-minute questions. "What if he see'd the hose? What if he knows I eated the Barbie heads?"

"Just tell him you have been good," I said. "Then you can tell him what you want for Christmas."

She opened her backpack and produced her book. She had glued pictures from catalogues on pieces of paper and tied them with string. "I give him this," she said.

"I think Santa Claus would like it better if you just told him," I said. "I don't think you should give him a whole book about your wishes."

She leaned over and whispered to me loudly: "I want him to see the pictures. I don't want him to have the elves make a Barbie for me. I want a *real* Barbie."

I started to get a little nervous. We were moving up in the line.

"Listen," I said, "just tell him what you want. If you tell him a Barbie, he'll know you mean the real Barbie."

"The elf Barbies can't look like real Barbies."

"I think they are real Barbies, yes," I said.

She thought about this. "Well, does Santa Claus put the Barbies in the stores?"

"I don't know." I looked around. "Maybe we should just leave and talk to him another time."

"No, I'll ask him. Do *you* put the Barbies in the store, Santa Claus? 'Cause *those* are the Barbies I want—not an elf kind of Barbie. I don't think that would make Santa Claus mad, do you?"

"I don't know." I stared straight ahead. Soon it was her turn. She climbed up on his lap, and he said, "Ho ho ho." I could see she was smiling stiffly as she handed him her book. She had two bright red splotches on her cheeks now that the moment had finally come. I saw her lean in and whisper something to him; he threw his head back and laughed at whatever it was. She said something again, and I heard him say, "Well, I don't know." Then together they looked through the pages quickly; she said something else, and he handed her a lollipop as the assistant snapped the picture. Then he put her down on the ground, and rolled his eyes at me.

She came back over to where I was standing. "Well?" I said. "Did you get everything answered?"

She wouldn't talk about it until we were in the car. "He wasn't the real Santa Claus," she said solemnly.

"He wasn't?"

"No. He didn't know I shared my cookie at day care. He pretended to be Santa Claus."

"Oh," I said.

"The real one was on the bus. Merember? *He* knows I shared my cookie."

"Well," I said. "That's good. You didn't ask him about the Barbies, did you?"

"I didn't even want to ask him. He didn't know anything about Santa Claus 'cause he's pretending."

Recently I came across the picture of her on Santa

Claus's lap. He's giving a fat, jolly smile in the direction of the camera, but she is frowning at him, no doubt thinking what a poor imitator he is. He's not even worth asking the hard questions of. At first I couldn't place the expression on her face, but then I realized who she looked like—Mike Wallace from *60 Minutes.*

6

Sitting Down to Supper and Jumping Up Again

Life at the dinner table

Nothing in your life thus far will prepare you for life at your dinner table now that you have a kid with some manual dexterity. When he was still a toddler, he hurled peas and Cheerios around the room *by accident* during mealtime, but now all that's changed. Now he can actually climb out of his Child Containment Device and deposit peas and Cheerios wherever he would like them to be—and life is never going to be the same. Even though you have very firm parental views on the necessity for staying in one's seat during the formal period of the day known as Dinnertime, so much stuff will happen around you that you're lucky if any of you spend more than ten consecutive seconds actually sitting on chairs.

My friend Ellen calls these the Magic Years because of the mysterious phenomena that are always swirling about a family in possession of a child between three and five. For instance, you'll all be sitting at the table, eating your various entrees (trust me, there will never be a time when you're all eating the same thing), and for no apparent reason, a bowl of broccoli will leap up in the air and slam down onto the floor. Just as you're running for towels and wondering at the fact that no one was even near the broccoli, a pork chop bone will go flying past your ear. The milk will spill. The tablecloth will start a slow shimmy off the end of the table, taking with it everyone's plates and silverware. The wallpaper will begin to curl at the corners.

"What I'd like to know," my husband said once, "is how it is that night after night at least four glasses of milk get spilled every time we sit down at the table, even though we only have three people, and you and I never spill anything."

"That's easy," I said. "We refill the kid's glass three times. Now, what *I'd* like to know is how the tablecloth—which has obediently stayed on the table throughout our entire marriage—now manages to work its way to the floor every dinnertime."

We agreed that we'd purchase a video camera and mount it above the table, so that we could later review the tapes and see just what the hell was taking place. But as with so many things when you have little kids, we never got either the money or the energy to go out and buy a video camera. And we certainly were too sleep deprived to trust ourselves to stand on ladders and try to mount something on the ceiling.

We gave up. You might as well, also.

Trust me on this one: no one with a little kid has ever liked mealtime. That is what you need to know, going in. That, and the fact that none of this is your fault.

Parents who say they enjoy dinnertimes with their small children are either lying, or else they are eating secretly in the kitchen after the kids have gone to bed. A friend of mine said he had always meant to try fasting while he was in college, and now that he had a three-year-old, he realized it was high time he got down to it. Other people have simply gone on the starvation diet, thinking that since everything looks so unappetizing anyway, why not take the opportunity to lose a few pounds?

Of course, whether you choose to take food by mouth or not, you will still be covered in it by the end of the meal, courtesy of your little one. There's not a child in the world who doesn't eat a few bites of food and then decide to regress back to his tiniest babyhood moments, when he expected a cuddle during his feeding. And so you will be sitting there, pushing some spaghetti around on your fork and praying that you can manage to get a few bites inserted before the next glass of milk falls into your plate, when there is your adorable, big-eyed little child, standing at your elbow and gazing up at you.

"I need lap," he'll say.

I don't know about you, but this would be the point where I'd get slightly hysterical, putting up a barrage of reasons why this was not a good time—begging, as it were, for a reprieve. "Please," I'd hear myself saying. "You can't sit on me because I have on my good clothes. Also I need two more bites of celery in order to keep myself from starving to death. And I just remembered I need to jump up and make a long distance telephone call to Cleveland in the next thirty seconds. Besides which I think the napkin on my lap is radioactive and if you sit on me, it could cause you to get cancer in later life."

This never works, of course, and before you know it, you have garlic bread smeared in your hair and spaghetti sauce across the front of your shirt. Your napkin is in shreds and there are saliva drops from your nose and cheeks, from the wet, open-mouthed kisses you've been blessed with.

Just think of it. Some people eat their dinner with no one to leap up and kiss them in the middle of the main course—and hardly ever do they get to sprint four times into the kitchen for yet another towel to wipe up cascading milk. And when they put a tablecloth on the table, it stays there. Oh, sure, it collects crumbs and has to be thrown into the washing machine every now and then. But you'll never see it suddenly start to slither into a puddle onto the floor.

These people are called childless people. You can recognize them out in the world because they never have garlic butter in their ears, and if they eat standing up in the kitchen at eleven at night, it's because the leftover beef burgundy with mushroom sauce was so delicious that they can't wait until tomorrow night to dine on the rest.

Yes, it's okay to hate them. You're just not allowed to throw things at them.

Okay, so here's the *real* story of dinner

It's not true that four glasses of milk will be spilled each and every time you sit down to dinner with your family. Nor will a bowl of broccoli suddenly leap up in the air and smash onto the floor. I made that part up. I even made up the part about the tablecloth falling on the floor every single night. In reality, it didn't happen more than once or twice a week, and not for any longer than five years even at that. And the broccoli bowl fell—I'm pretty sure of this now—only because my child kept tugging on the tablecloth little by little until the bowl reached the edge and slid off.

Also, there are people who actually do sit down at the table each evening with their kids, who wouldn't dream of going on starvation diets or eating in the kitchen later. One friend of mine, Leslie, says she looks forward to dinnertime each night because it's the time she can teach her little children about manners.

"I tell them we can only have polite conversation then, and that we have to eat all our food, and put our napkins in our laps—stuff like that," she told me.

"What did you talk about at the table last night?" I asked.

"Oh, well. Last night," she said, laughing. "Last night wasn't our best night."

"No, really. What did you talk about?"

"We talked about how it wasn't good dinner-table talk to bring up poop and pee."

I laughed.

"We actually had an entire dinner devoted to the idea that people *shouldn't* talk about poop at the dinner table. There were lots of issues to be decided: can you never even *mention* poop and pee? What if someone in your class went pee in his pants that day at school, and your parent wants to know what happened at school? Since that's the main thing that happened, are you allowed to mention it? And what about baby poops? Can those be talked about?"

"You mean poops from the new baby?"

"Those, or historical ones from the past. Times of diarrhea. Trips to restaurant potties. Especially horrible-looking potties we'd seen in public places. We went over it all, believe me."

You see, this is the state of the American dinner hour today, even from people who are so mentally healthy they are able to think about manners. So you must not feel bad if things aren't going so well at your own dinner table, on any given night. Here's what you can expect at a typical dinnertime:

- You will get up at least six times to cut your child's meat into yet *smaller* pieces. The steak will finally be so small it requires a microscope to find some of the pieces on the plate.
- Two foods will at some point touch each other on the plate, rendering both inedible. You will find yourself arguing that only the *edges* of the food should be thought of as inedible. Surely the centers are just as pure and pristine as they had

been and can be eaten without any danger of con-
tamination.

- Your child will drop her fork on the floor at least
  three times. The third time, you will rouse yourself out of your inertia to remember that germs
  are bad, and go get a new fork out of the drawer.
  It will then drop as well.
- The salt will fall over, a spoonful of something
  gross will fall to the floor, the milk will spill at least
  twice. At least seven other times the glass will be
  bumped in such a way that it totters on its axis
  for up to six seconds, forcing you to hold your
  breath each time.
- You will make at least two statements per dinnertime that you never thought you'd hear yourself
  say—things like, "Don't stick your fingers in the
  butter after you've been petting the dog" or "If
  you're going to lick your knife, make sure it's not
  the serrated one."
- You will say the words, "Come on, one bite won't
  kill you" at least ten times.
- You will say the words, "Don't feed the dog peas
  from the table. Dogs don't like peas."
- You will say, "Tell me something that happened at
  school today," just to make polite conversation,
  and then, once the story of little Calvin Turner's
  nosebleed gets going, you'll wish that you hadn't.

The pasta years—and years and years

When kids get past their third birthday, you might expect
that their diets will improve some. You want to see an end
to those years of eating lunches consisting of one beetle,
half a peanut-butter cookie, and three tablespoons of mus-

tard washed down with some red punch. It's time, you say, that they paid attention to what is and is not Real Food. Just for starters, you'd like to see them give up the kind of stuffing that comes inside teddy bears and switch to Stove Top.

This doesn't happen overnight, of course. Once they've given up dryer lint mixed with some duck sauce packets from the Chinese take-out place, they go through a fairly extensive transition period when nothing passes through their lips that isn't some sort of noodle.

At first you'll be happy about this. Unlike the wrappers on crayons, noodles are listed in the government's Food Pyramid—and although no one would recommend that they be the sole provider of nutrition, at least your child is eating something that has genuine organic components that one can use as fuel. And, you think, with a few added ingredients here and there—perhaps a branch of broccoli, for instance—someday this noodle situation could approach something like a balanced meal.

Do not get your expectations too high. At this stage in life, it's best not to hope for too much. For one thing, most children will accept noodle toppings only if they are: (1) the same basic color as the noodles, (2) ten times slimier, and (3) raise the cholesterol value of the meal by 300 percent.

This, of course, can only mean butter. And certain kinds of cheeses.

You might as well forget right now about putting any green thing on a noodle. Certainly vegetables have no place mixing with pasta, but even spices are not to be tolerated. Children reject all spices on the grounds that they might wreck the delicate cardboard flavor of plain noodles. Besides, it can be aesthetically displeasing to see little dark specks on a pure white noodle. No one should have to put up with that. It disturbs the pristine, snowy terrain of the pasta landscape.

I have seen a whole plate of spaghetti rendered inedible because a stray flake of oregano, perhaps wafting through the air from the adult plate, somehow maneuvered itself onto a child's noodle strand. You would need either a magnifying glass or a pair of four-year-old eyes to be able to see this speck, mind you. But your child swears that it is there, and he is certain it has contaminated the entire meal, and maybe some other meals as well. Perhaps nothing else will ever be able to be eaten on this plate again, due to this unfortunate circumstance.

Some parents have thought that spaghetti sauce would be okay on a noodle because of tradition (spaghetti has traditionally been served with red tomato sauce, after all; it's sort of part of the definition of the word "spaghetti"). Also, tomato sauce has a very fortuitous resemblance to ketchup (a perennial favorite). But studies among four-year-olds have shown that spaghetti sauce is, in fact, good *only* when it's not touching a piece of pasta. Spaghetti sauce, which is already a suspect food because of being loaded with little green specks and sometimes the Dreaded Onion, can only be consumed in the most unorthodox fashion possible— like licking it up off the floor, for instance.

No, you will find that pasta is acceptable only when it's in its plain, unadorned form—boiled until all the last nutritional component is out of it, and then plopped into a bowl. Once, on a particularly bad day, I came into the kitchen to find my child eating macaroni noodles out of the box.

"That's supposed to be cooked before you eat it," I said.

"I like it this way," she said. "It's like crackers."

Then why, I wanted to say, don't you eat crackers?

But there's no need to get into such inflammatory questions. Nutrition is nutrition, after all. Even if it's a raw noodle.

Purple mashed potatoes

Kids come in two types: those who eat everything in sight and then find it necessary to supplement by snacking on the couch pillows after polishing off a seven-course dinner— and those who take one lick of a candy cane all day long and declare they're too full to eat any more.

I don't know why nature couldn't have issued us little people who appreciate the wonders of food, but not too much—and who are grateful and hungry, yet restrained, when we put dishes of it in front of them. But apparently this would violate some design specification for small humans, because I have never met a kid who ate that way. Instead, you're either hiding food from them because they can eat their way through a whole crate of Fritos while you're on a thirty-second call with a telemarketer, or else you're whining and pleading for them to eat just one "itty bitty teensy weensy bite of muffin—just try it! Just one little bite, for God's sake! Would it kill you to eat just one crumb?"

It is this latter kind of desperation, I'm afraid, that will one day lead you to purple mashed potatoes.

You'll soon realize that pleading for food consumption is wrong, that it alarms kids when you invoke both God and death in the name of persuading them to eat a bite of something they would probably like anyway, if only they would just try it. I think it's best to save God and the forces of death for asparagus or Brussels sprouts. For muffins, you can pretty much leave them on the table and walk away, and generally, if the child doesn't perceive that you would get a whole lot of satisfaction if he ate it—well, then he might sample it. And that could lead to some substantial calorie intake.

But be warned: the evening will come when you are whipping up some delectable mashed potatoes from scratch—something you never had when you were a kid. Your own mother only served boxes of mashed potato flakes, and it wasn't until you were well into your teens that you realized that a mashed potato actually came from those brown, rock-looking things in the grocery store. (French fries, too.) Anyway, you will be standing there, slaving over the billows of potatoes—and you realize heavily that nothing you say or do will persuade your child to try these.

Oh, sure, they're the same color as macaroni, which should have a soothing effect. But you know that won't work. They're the wrong consistency. Potatoes are going to look to your child like a suspicious, foreign substance. Of course mashed potatoes could be compared to ice cream— you might want to invoke that comparison. But that would be the wrong way to go. Potatoes are warm and lumpy, and they can't win in a contest against ice cream. Best not even to bring it up.

That's when you realize with a sinking heart that no one under the height of five feet tall is going to eat those mashed potatoes. And so you search wildly for something that would make them appealing. Certainly nothing you can *add* to them will help: this would violate the Food Touching Other Food Rule.

And that's when you might do what my friend Cindy did. In desperation, she reached for the food coloring and turned the mashed potatoes bright red.

Blood red.

"It looked," she said later, "like something that had come directly from the operating room. My husband was looking at me like I'd lost my mind."

Naturally her kids wouldn't touch it. Who would? So she got up and added blue food coloring and made them purple.

"This is purple mountain's majesty, above the fruited plain," she announced, a little desperately.

"I don't eat mountings magistry," her four-year-old insisted.

"And I don't eat any fruit airplane," said her five-year-old.

Cindy and her husband managed to choke down a few bites before deciding to throw out the entire experiment. Three months later, she told all of us at the playground that she realized where she went wrong.

"It's not enough to turn them another color," she said. "You have to rename them something disgusting as well."

If she'd only insisted that the red mashed potatoes *were* brains left over from the surgical floor, she said, her kids would have gobbled them right up.

Fourteen known ways of making macaroni and cheese

It seems simple enough. Your child only wants to eat macaroni and cheese, and so you feed it to her. How hard can this be? Why, a person could even go to a restaurant and order it off the menu. Theoretically, that is.

For some reason, this doesn't work. My friend Beth, who has three boys, has documented the fact that even in a family where *only* macaroni and cheese is ever consumed, fixing it is still as complicated as making Thanksgiving dinner for seventy people, thirty of whom are vegetarians and twenty of whom insist on sausage stuffing for the turkey.

There are, she insists, fourteen ways of making macaroni and cheese, and she has spent much of her recent life in the kitchen trying to find one way that each person in her family would eat. This was fruitless. After exhaustive research, it has been determined that in a family of five, on any given night you can make no fewer than three different

kinds of macaroni and cheese—that is, if you want everyone
to eat it.

- Macaroni noodles (must be elbows), with grated
  orange American cheese sprinkled over the top.
  No other substance, even salt, can be permitted.
- Elbows prepared with a roux of American and
  Cheddar cheese, then baked in the oven with buttered bread crumbs sprinkled on top.
- Elbows baked with the roux—that's okay, but if
  there's even one whiff of bread crumbs in there,
  forget it. In fact, that "other kind" of macaroni
  must not have been prepared in the same oven.
- Macaroni with cold slabs of American cheese
  spread across the top. The cheese, of course, must
  be soft, but not melted.
- Macaroni with cold clumps of Parmesan cheese
  sprinkled on top.
- Kraft macaroni and cheese. Made strictly according to package directions.
- Kraft macaroni and cheese, but with only the macaroni noodles themselves being cooked. The
  yummy neon-colored cheese powder must be consumed separately through a straw or with a moistened index finger.
- Macaroni with white Cheddar cheese, cut into
  chunks, disguised among the noodles. If any
  chunk of cheese is visible, must be made over.
- Macaroni prepared at least twenty-four hours in
  advance, kept in the refrigerator, and then
  served with warm orange cheese poured over
  the top. But not so much cheese that the noodles get warm. And it's cheating if you heat the
  cheese in the microwave because all the oil rises
  to the top.

- Hot macaroni with mozzarella cheese on top. (The cheese must make a long string from the plate to the eater's mouth, or it will be suspected of not being true mozzarella.)
- Macaroni made with cold cream cheese stirred into it.
- A bowl of warm milk with macaroni and chunks of orange cheese floating in it.
- Raw macaroni noodles, eaten crunchy-style, with Cheez-Its on the side. (In some circles, Cheez-Its are considered to be of the same nutritional value as cheese.)
- Macaroni and cottage cheese.

When kids cook

Every now and then you'll meet a parent who is obviously from another planet. That's the only possible explanation for how put-together they are. Anyway, that's the way I felt when I first met Julie at the park. Immediately I knew she was going to be someone worth listening to.

First of all, she had four children, while I only had one. And she was wearing lipstick actually *on* her lips and not on her cheeks or on her shirt. Best of all, unlike the other mothers in my group, she did not look as though she had been crying recently. She came to the park each day equipped with sand toys, sunscreen, and plenty of healthy sandwiches that her children *devoured* at lunchtime without even once whining at her for bringing the wrong thing. I think it's possible they even threw their wrappers away in the park trash cans.

The rest of us were in immediate awe of her, and it wasn't long before she was telling us her secrets.

The first one, she said firmly, was to delegate authority.

"You can't do everything yourself," she said. "That's the main thing."

We knew she meant husbands, and many of us already had husbands who were doing what was said to be their share. They changed diapers, threw toddlers into the air and gave them piggyback rides, and knew their way around a can of soup. This wasn't the '50s, for God's sake, when a woman had to whisper the children's names to her husband before they trooped in to kiss him good night behind his newspaper.

But no. Julie was not really talking about delegating to the husbands. It was beyond her worldview that husbands weren't already doing half the housework.

"The kids," she told us. "The kids have to do their own laundry, clean their rooms. And of course, they must take their turn at fixing meals each week."

We gasped and looked over at our three-year-olds happily hitting one another with plastic trucks. *Them? Laundry? Cooking?*

"They can do it," she said firmly. "My little Bradley (Bradley was three and a half at the time) knows that Tuesday is his night to fix dinner, and we all eat whatever Bradley fixes us."

"But I don't really *like* worm innards and dirt cakes," said one woman.

"Oh, that's just at first," said Julie. "Then they settle down and really start making meals."

"Like what does Bradley make on his night?" I asked.

"Well," she said, "last Tuesday we had carrots, Velveeta cheese, and leftover Easter eggs."

We had to admit that several of your major food groups were represented in that meal—which was better than had been the case at my house, where, I believe, we had had buttered noodles. I had actually put a bowl of raw carrots on the table as well, but much of that landed on the floor and was eaten by the dog. And the rest I found in one of the kids' milk glasses when I went to rinse the dishes.

Kids cooking! It was such a heady idea. Why, the self-esteem they would garner from being one of the meal pre-parers! The time off *I* would have! Plus, they would have to think up the meals, and as everybody knows, that's really the worst of dinner. Once someone tells you, "Okay, let's have Easter eggs and Velveeta cheese," the rest is easy. It's the thinking part that's so tough.

So I went home and explained to my little ones, ages six and three, that they were now in charge of an evening meal each week. The little one cried.

"No, no!" I said. "This is *good*. You can fix anything you want, and we'll all eat it. You'll be in charge."

She wiped her eyes and looked at me suspiciously. "We eat what I say?"

"Yes!" I said. "Anything but dirt and rocks from outside, okay? It has to be food."

For a minute I thought we were going to have our old argument: Are Grass Cuttings Food? But then she just smiled and went off to play, secure in knowing she didn't have to fix dinner for four more days. It was a feeling I envied.

On my night, I made lamb chops, mint jelly, mashed potatoes, and butternut squash. My husband fixed cheese-burgers, potato chips, and green salad on his night. The six-year-old, after spending most of the afternoon in the kitchen, came out with bowls of Cheerios loaded with sugar, an unopened can of fruit cocktail (he couldn't work the can opener), and celery sticks.

The little one served up some plain slices of Wonder bread, asking that we participate by cutting off the crusts for everyone; a gallon of grape Juicy juice, which she suggested we dunk our bread slices into; and a bag of frozen corn, which she said were to be eaten "the good way, like Popsicles."

After dinner, my husband cried.

The experiment limped on for a few more weeks, with the lasting result that frozen corn became a major staple of my family's dinner menus. It was when the three-year-old started insisting that the frozen corn be served nightly in the Champagne flutes that I realized we were in deeper than I was ready for, and went back to being the family cook.

I think Julie's kids by now have become gourmet chefs with their own cooking shows on the Food Network. But we're still eating frozen corn some nights, although I have never—I repeat, *never*—willingly dunked a piece of crustless Wonder bread into Juicy juice of any flavor. I just want you to know that.

Worm blood stew—or the joys of renaming foods

When I was a little kid, being difficult on the subject of food, my father once tried to convince me to eat a bowl of tapioca pudding by telling me those were little fish eyes floating there in the milkiness.

I still remember the shock going through me. "Fish eyes?" I cried. *"Fish eyes?"* And being prone to loud, dramatic scenes, I fell to the floor, writhing and screaming in horror, while he shrugged, finished up the rest of the tapioca pudding, and went outside to mow the lawn.

For years I always thought that fish-eye story was just a clever way for him to get my pudding away from me and eat it for himself. But now that I'm a mother, I can see what he was really doing.

He was being a guy.

You see, my father was raised in the kind of household

where the males outnumbered the females three to one, and so he thought *everybody* not wanting to eat their tapioca pudding might be thinking that pudding is too boring to fool with. He was doing what boys love most—renaming food to make it more interesting.

It wasn't until I grew up and had a little boy myself that I discovered you could get them to eat any number of things by simply telling them it was something hideous. I still don't know why a male will so happily dive in to beef stew if he thinks he's getting some monster intestines mixed with eyeball jelly, but there you have it. It's the one surefire way to get a boy to eat whatever you want him to.

This method, however, doesn't work on most girls I know. A little girl beyond the age of, say, three years old, won't intentionally eat a yucky thing. Before that, you will see her outside snacking on snails, furious to realize that she can't get her tongue to completely remove all the soft snail material in the shell. But all that quickly changes. One day she wakes up in the morning and refuses to eat anything that doesn't have a written guarantee of food authenticity, and a pretty name as well.

I once spent an afternoon making spinach dumplings, a project that turned out to be way more work than I had bargained for. And it was with a sinking heart that I realized no one was actually going to eat them, that I might as well have opened a can of ravioli instead and spent the afternoon reading novels and polishing my toenails.

I devoted my time to thinking of how I would present these dumplings to the family. My son, I figured, would eat them if I called them Frankenstein Eyeballs. I could claim the green specks of spinach were green veins and arteries.

But my daughter—she was going to be the tricky one. She needed a name that was both elegant and delicious, that communicated the subtle power of an ingredient she already liked, as well as the personality of a cartoon character and a food she could relate to.

The answer—which I had to tell her in the kitchen so the other two couldn't hear—was "Butter Popeye Pastries."

We polished off the entire batch. Sometimes it works and sometimes it doesn't.

7

Four Years Old:
All That I Am,
I Owe to My Preschool

Life in the theater of the absurd

Four-year-olds, no longer hampered by the insecurities that plagued them when they were mere babies of three, are now fully ready to take over the world. They just have to fight a few pirates on the playground first and maybe deal with a Tyrannosaurus rex or two in the block corner. Oh, and would you mind agreeing to be Pocahontas's grandmother and standing perfectly still in the backyard for about an hour holding on to a willow tree branch? You *would* mind? Well, okay, then, you can be a bulldozer driver and pretend you're stopping in a diner for lunch, and your child is the waitress who will say she's out of every food you request.

Living with a four-year-old, I've decided, is a cross between living in someone else's series of one-act plays and being in a witness protection program. You never know what identity you'll have to assume next. In one Sunday afternoon, I once had to be a butcher delivering hot dogs, a patient yelping over a series of painful injections, Santa Claus's best elf (my daughter was his acting-out, rebellious elf whom I was sent to chastise), a woman yelling at the garbage man not to throw garbage on the grass, a nursery school teacher who stuttered, and a shoe saleswoman who was trying to sell a pair of broken shoes.

It's no wonder that parents of four-year-olds always have that deer-in-the-headlights look about them and often can't remember their own real names. They are waiting to see what character they have to play next, and just hoping it's a role they can slip into while they perhaps get dinner on the table.

But here's the other hard part about being the parent of a four-year-old, the unexpectedly bad part. No one, absolutely no one, will sympathize with you. When you go out among adults—assuming you're eligible for a pass or have thought to secure necessary employment for yourself outside the home—you'll find yourself met with blank stares when you start to explain about your new acting responsibilities at home.

People without children—or those who have older children but have forgotten what real life is like—will tell you that if you don't *want* to play the role of a bulldozer operator with a broken leg, you can just say no.

"Studies have shown that it's good for kids to hear the word no every now and then," said one friend of mine. "And anyway, children must learn to play on their own and entertain themselves."

This is all very well and good when you're out at the office thinking about the unfortunate direction your life has gone, but like a lot of child-rearing theories, it just doesn't stand up when you're actually in the moment. You *know* it's good to say no every now and then; what the advice givers don't seem to realize is that you have said no to approximately forty-five things since breakfast that morning. Besides that, you have to admit you're rather charmed that your child is playing creatively instead of simply zoning out in front of the television set.

The answer, I'm afraid, is more children.

Don't worry. You don't have to make more children yourself—although the theory of having multiple kids because they will eventually entertain one another has gotten a lot of good press and does sometimes work. But in this instance, by the time you could run upstairs with your spouse, start a new baby, gestate it, give birth to it, and wait for it to want to play Bulldozer Operator, chances are the older child would be sick of that game and would be looking around for someone to play jacks with or something. And then you'll still have to play, because if you don't, your older child will very likely end up feeding jacks to your younger child if you try to leave them alone together.

No, here's what you want to do. You want to go to the telephone and call someone else's kid over for a play date.

I know that at first it may seem counter-intuitive to introduce even *more* kids to the scene going on at your house. You figure that if you are barely hanging on with one child in the vicinity, you'll be pushed over the line into seeking out illegal pharmaceuticals if you let kids start to outnumber you. Just try to relax and take some deep breaths. For reasons no one can quite discern, two children of four years are very often half as much trouble as one child of four.

This is because usually one of them is willing to be the waitress and one the customer, and they will have a splendid, if intense, time shouting at each other about the menu selections—and then, in a flash, the game will change and one of them will be a crotchety grandmother and the other a flamboyant dancing pig, way faster than you could have ever made the mental adjustment.

When you're in the company of a couple of playing-well-together four-year-olds, all you hear is negotiations for scenes.

"Okay," says one child, "let's pretend you're the bad guy, and I'm the dog at the fire station."

"I don't want to be a bad guy," says the other.

"Well, you're a good guy but some people *think* you're a bad guy."

"I want to be just a good guy and everybody knows it."

"Well, those people are *wrong* who think you're a bad guy, because you *are* a good guy."

"Okay. Let's pretend I'm a pirate."

"Pirates are bad guys."

"Let's pretend I'm a good guy pirate."

"There's no such thing as a good guy pirate. Pirates are always bad."

"Well, I'm not bad. I'm the kind of pirate who gives boat rides to kids."

"Okay, let's pretend you give boat rides to kids, and I'm a dog who eats kids."

"Okay, let's pretend I'm on the boat, and the dog bites me, and I push him in the water."

"And then let's pretend the dog jumps in the water and chases you and eats you up."

"And let's pretend I kill the dog with a big stick like this—"

Oh, there's just one other thing: Sometimes when there's another kid around, you have to step in and use your life-saving techniques. But hey—at least *you're* not having to play the part of the rabid dog jumping in the water and biting a pirate. That's a consoling thought.

Peer pressure

Besides saving lives among good friends who will happily maim each other in the name of dramatic authenticity, you will find you also have to wade into the sticky waters of peer pressure when you're among four-year-olds.

You might not have been expecting peer pressure to show up for several years—not until teenagerhood, if you're the type who believes what you read in the papers and see on situation comedies on television. But the truth is that probably even babies worry that they're not like the other babies. I believe I have detected pacifier envy among very young infants, but luckily for the rest of us they don't have the verbal skills to ask that you replace their inferior plugs with the newly discovered deluxe model that Baby Timmy is chewing on. And so even though they're crying about their lack of adequate pacifiers, you probably think they're crying just because they're wet and hungry or the air currents in the room have disturbed them somehow.

But now that they're four, they can talk and explain to you just how vital it is to have a green shirt like Cameron's and a truck like Brett's. They do this with all the earnestness of a social worker. "I *need* a green shirt because people don't like me in my purple shirt," a four-year-old kid will say, and you will feel your jaw slacken in disbelief.

"What do you mean, people don't like you? Everyone thinks you look handsome in your purple shirt."

"They think I should wear green like Cameron does."

"Who exactly thinks this? I want their names and phone numbers."

Your child looks at you, as though trying to figure out if this is simply another of your ploys to get out of doing what he wants, and then—using the Broken Record technique that is recommended by all sales agencies in the United States—says patiently, "I want a green shirt. I want a green shirt. I want a green shirt. I want a green shirt."

The answer, of course, is No. You don't want to start buying clothes just because Cameron's mother happened onto a green shirt sale. Nor do you want your child dressing like somebody else just because he thinks it would enhance his standing in the nursery school community. You flash back to a certain denim jacket and some foolishly trimmed bellbottom jeans, but weren't you about fifteen when you couldn't live without those? And what did *your* mother say?

For the first time in your life, you are tempted to ask

the age-old question: If Cameron jumped off a bridge in his green shirt, would that mean that you would have to jump off, too?

Later it turns out that, green shirts aside, everybody who *is* anybody in preschool is wearing a superhero cape these days. Even the teacher has mentioned to you that it would be helpful if you could just manage to rustle up a cape for those early-morning free play sessions where *all* the kids rush around saving the world.

"When your child doesn't have a cape," she explains to you, using her delicate voice that indicates so much happening just beneath the surface, "well, then, *he* has to be the one who's getting rescued. And I don't think you want to have that be a pattern in life."

God forbid your kid develops a Need of Rescue complex. You search the stores until you find a wonderful, delightful superhero's cape, and while you're at it, a green shirt that your son says is just like Cameron's.

Oh, well. He needed a new shirt anyhow.

"Don't get into the shower with Mr. Jordan!"

One thing about four-year-olds is that they are always on the lookout for ways of making life more interesting. This, after all, is really their chief job in life. Now that the challenges of walking and creating human speech are mastered yet it's still not time to move on to calculus and astrophysics, they spend quite a bit of time devising ways to make *your* life and theirs fuller, richer, and generally more harrowing.

This is where the imaginary friend has so much to contribute.

It's sad, if you think about it too hard, that a kid finally realizes that she herself cannot wreak enough havoc personally and has to subcontract out some of the troublemaking. But there you have it: it's the twenty-first century now, and we've all had to realize our limitations. So if your child has developed a relationship with an imaginary person and that makes it possible for her to meet her daily quota for fun, merriment, and parent yanking, then I say more power to her.

You, on the other hand, will have nothing but fun with the imaginary friend. For some reason, friends from the unseen world are always inserting themselves in the chair you are about to sit in, and causing your child to screech in alarm every time you sit down anywhere. Imaginary friends don't like the food you cook, they rile up your own darling child at bedtime, and they generally do so many wicked things in a day that you grow quite tired of hearing about their adventures. Once, I was about to get in the shower and my child informed me that a certain Mr. Jordan was already in the shower and would be out in a minute. Until then I hadn't been familiar with the work of Mr. Jordan.

"You just have to wait for the shower because he's very shy," she said to me.

We both listened to the water running. I was thinking that the hot water was running down the drain while I was standing there, shivering, waiting to get in, and for no good reason—and she was explaining that with Mr. Jordan being so shy and all, it wouldn't be good to startle him in the shower.

"When he gets scared, he does awful things," she said ominously.

"Tell him he needs to get out now," I said, "because I've got to get to work."

"Mr. Jordan! Mr. Jordan!" she called into the tub. "I'm afraid my mommy is in a big hurry." She cocked her head, listening for a moment. "He said to tell you he's extra dirty today, and it might take a little bit longer. A skunk got into his hair."

I got in the shower anyway.

She cried.

"It's okay!" I yelled to her from under the running water. "I'm helping Mr. Jordan get all the skunk stuff out of his hair. He's very happy I'm in here with him."

"I'll just bet he is," came my husband's voice from the hallway. "Now, *who* did you say is in there with you?"

As if that wasn't bad enough, later I discovered the trash cans in the bedrooms had all been overturned. Mr. Jordan had apparently gone on an embarrassed rampage and needed to let off a little bit of steam.

"Mr. Jordan was very mad at you," said my daughter. "I tried to tell him not to do any bad things, but he wouldn't listen."

"I'll tell him myself," I said. "Where is he?"

"He's sitting on the stove, turning on the buttons," she said.

"Mr. Jordan, you stop that right this minute!" I said in the direction of the stove. "If you can't behave like a normal human being, you are going to have to take a time-out in the living room. We do not allow people to act like that around here, do you understand me? Think of the example you're setting for the rest of us, do you hear?"

My daughter was smiling at me.

"Well," I said finally, "I think I got things clear to Mr. Jordan. I don't think he'll be giving us any more trouble."

"Mr. Jordan," said my daughter sweetly, "left when he heard you say 'Stop it right this minute!' He said to tell you he went out to play."

I said it would be great if Mr. Jordan would just stay out to play forever since he'd been regularly complaining about the food and never wanted anything to eat other than candy and fruit roll-ups.

She gave me a long look. "You know what Mr. Jordan

says about you? He says you're not the best mommy he ever saw."

"Oh, yeah?" I said. "Well, then why doesn't he go back to his own mommy's house if things aren't so good for him here?"

"Maybe he will!"

"Good!"

My husband came through the kitchen about that time and gave me a strange look. Later that night, after our daughter had gone upstairs to bed, he said gently, "Maybe we don't want to waste our best ammunition, you know, on a fellow that's not even really there."

"That's easy for *you* to say," I told him. "But I happen to know that right now you're sitting on Mr. Jordan's head, and *he is not happy.*"

Politics on the playground

You're not the only one who's baffled by what takes place on the playground. Oh, sure, you know something about the toys—the sandbox, the swings, the buckets and shovels and tricycles. You may even have a handle on the slide, the baby dolls lying facedown in the mud, and the climbing structure.

Ha! That is all nothing—*nothing*—compared to the real story of what's taking place there. What looks like innocent child's play is actually a complicated system of social intrigue and backroom politics, with judges, juries, and lawyers on hand to rule on all the millions of infractions that occur. There are, studies have shown, more rules and regulations in the sandbox than there are in some of your major corporations. The only difference is that in the sandbox, there isn't any E-mail and no office Christmas parties.

Unlike just a year or so ago, when everybody played alongside one another but didn't interact, now everybody's paying close attention to everyone else. This is so they can immediately know if anything *unfair* is happening around them. Seeking out unfairness is the most time-consuming job that four-year-olds have, and they take it very seriously. It is *unfair*, for instance, if little Bethany holds on to the one-legged baby doll longer than Delilah got to hold on to it, and *massively unfair* if Delilah starts crying and Bethany then swings the doll around by its only leg, and chants, "Nah nah nah nah *nah* nah! I've got the baby and *yoooooooo* do-on't!"

Now, here's the difference between adults and kids. Here are the following things an adult would say to solve this situation:

- "Delilah and Bethany, play nice."
- "Delilah, stop being a baby."
- "Bring that baby doll over here and I'll fix it."
- "Who cares about that old broken baby anyway? Why don't you play with blocks instead?"
- "Bethany, you're going to put somebody's eye out with that baby doll's leg."
- "Delilah, if you can't stop crying, you're going to have to go to a time-out."
- "Okay, everybody, time for naps!"

Children, however, would be immediately concerned with rectifying the injustice that had taken place, and they would be attuned to every one of the subtleties, based on past history, the psychological profiles of the children involved, and probably some climatic variations in wind currents as well. For instance, they would need to first make sure that Bethany wasn't about to break the one good baby doll leg, since that would escalate the crime from a simple misdemeanor to a possible sandbox felony offense. Then someone would be appointed to comfort Delilah (all the adult could think of was yelling at her), while another committee would be dispatched to reason with Bethany, with an eye toward a possible violent overthrow and tackling to get the doll, if necessary. Someone else, the leader who often functions as the group psychiatrist, would be in charge of making pronouncements about what is happening—explaining loudly to the group exactly what is going on and assigning the tasks.

Later, if left alone, the children would have a discussion on the more global issue that showed up in the situation: should kids themselves enforce time limits on Baby Doll Usage, and if so, how long is just right?

No one would suggest that everybody go for naps, believe me.

I once listened, stunned, as a group of children in nursery school discussed the fair way of passing food at the table. Someone had requested seconds on muffins at snack time, and a few children helped themselves to a second muffin as the basket made its way down the table to the original requestor. Was this *fair*, everyone wanted to know.

One boy, who was approximately two feet tall and weighed in at about twenty-two pounds, piped up that it wasn't fair for people to pick out muffins first because the Original Requestor might not then get the muffin of her choice, and since she was the one who had thought of asking, she had first dibs. (First dibs is the cornerstone of fairness, you will realize when you hang out with four-year-olds.)

But then somebody else pointed out that that wasn't exactly *fair* to pick out the best and biggest and most luscious muffin for yourself anyhow—so what did it matter if other people grabbed one on the way down the table? This faction believed that there was no criminal intent as long as there was still a muffin left by the time the basket made its way to the Original Requestor.

Frankly, I hadn't seen this much dedication to the concept of fairness since my aerobics class tried to divide a lunch check after two of us just had plain tea and the rest had had yogurt smoothies. And even then, the concept of global fairness may have been missing.

The witness protection program— or the new regime of daily life

It's when they're four that you get your first real glimpse of the fact that they have definite ideas about who they want to be. The first thing they have to do to establish this brand-new identity is to get rid of that old, boring, useless name you gave them.

My son woke me up in the middle of the night once to announce that he hated the name Benjamin and had chosen a new name for himself.

In those days, I was instantly wide awake upon being told *anything* in the middle of the night. My kids have always been in training for night watchman jobs, I think, and so the middle of the night was when they were awake and wandering through the house, musing over life's little conundrums. I was used to having long, complex, and sleepy discussions about the circulatory system, the uses of the internal combustion engine, and why people are called human beans.

But a name change! "I think Benjamin is a wonderful name," I told him. "It's one of my favorite names."

"Well," he said, "I'm tired of it. I don't like it anymore."

"Okay," I said. "Well, I'll see you in the morning. Good night."

"But don't you want to know my new name?"

I braced myself for Fireman Frank or Spiderman or Wildcat Jones or any of those names that have a little pizzazz to them. But instead, he said, "Now I'm Herman."

After he trotted back to bed, I lay there awake trying to think of where this might have come from. Was there a terrific Herman anywhere in our lives? No, of course not. Ben was born during the era when kids were being named Jeremy or Hunter or Tree. There hadn't been a Herman born in southern California for at least thirty years. Who ever knows where these things come from? Luckily for me, he forgot his new name almost as soon as he had given it to himself. By morning, he was Ben again.

It wasn't so easy when my daughters decided to change their names. One became Bella Lissima and was steadfast in her quest to be called that full-time. One day, after I'd made about seventy-two mistakes with her name, she quietly told me, "I'm sorry, but from now on, I can't really answer you unless you call me Bella Lissima." And she didn't.

The other, who was under the influence of a sophisticated friend in second grade, decided her real name was her own name spelled backward. We had to call her Nosilla Yma for two straight weeks, up until the point that her brother nicknamed her Nostrilla Yma, and then she wanted to go back to Allison.

A pooster is a kid who's crying for his mother

One of the main advantages to being the parent of a four-year-old, besides the fact that you learn to wake up at the drop of a whisper, is that you learn a whole lot of new words. If we truly had our wits about us in this country, we would have little children writing the language, because they really know which words are the good ones.

One day my daughter got in the car after nursery school and announced that she would not be marrying the guy she'd been planning on. He had been a good candidate, in my opinion: he was good with the crayons *and* markers (shows versatility), always shared the tricycles with her when they were outside (generosity as well as respect for women), and could dance like Michael Jackson (a sense of fun—this was before Michael Jackson got in such trouble).

But no, she said. There was one huge problem with him.

"What is that?" I asked.

"He's a pooster," she said.

"Did you say a rooster?"

"Nope, he's a pooster. Just a pooster."

"And, uh, what might a pooster be?"

"A pooster," she said patiently, "is somebody who cries for his mommy."

Since then, I see poosters wherever I go, and now that I have a word for them, I've been able to point them out to others as well. Poosterism is rampant these days in all walks of life, and it sounds so much more descriptive to use that term than to simply call people whiners.

Kids are the best namers there are. My sister, at four, always referred to hot dogs as "little rascals" because *The Little Rascals* TV show was sponsored by a hot dog company. It took us a long time to figure out what she was talking about when she kept asking for little rascals for lunch, but once we caught on to it, we could see that this was actually the right name for hot dogs. They *are* little rascals, after all, with all that fat and sodium.

She's also the one who got us calling squirrels "trenches." We were at the park one day when she pointed to some squirrels, and asked, "Are those the kind of trenches that go on the collars of trench coats?"

You can't come up with words any better than that. True,

people will stare at you when you start to refer to things the way your children do, but that's one advantage to being a parent. You get a whole new secret language, one that most other people can't figure out.

My four-year-old daughter one day was drinking orange juice when she suddenly yelled, "Oh! Now I see why they call it Tropicana!"

"Why?" I said.

"Because they take the oranges, and they *trop* them up and throw them in the *canna*!"

A person *could* start to explain about the word "chop," I suppose, and the word "can" and all manner of things having to do with orange juice production. But let me tell you what is more likely to happen instead: you nod and smile, and the next time you are drinking Tropicana orange juice, you will smile.

And when someone outside your family asks you what's so funny, you might attempt to explain about the Tropicana tropping and canning industry. But after one try, you'll learn, and you'll just say, "Oh . . . nothing."

Do yourself a favor: don't tell every pooster all the new words you've learned. They have to get their own little rascals.

Birthday parties

I have to tell you more about birthday parties.

They are not fun for parents. Take it from me: no parent has ever finished presiding over a child's birthday party and said, "Wow, that was so much fun I can't wait until next year!" Most parents are lucky if they can limp to their beds for a long-term nap before they need to start the demolition work on the house. And here's the worst part: as bad as it was to throw a birthday party for your three-year-old, that was nothing—*nothing*—compared to what happens when you're giving a birthday party for your four-year-old.

When they're three, they're still impressed simply by the fact that people are coming to their house and bringing presents. Basically, they think the whole day was a wonderful idea, even if they did throw a couple of tantrums and hurl cake at the windows. But four-year-olds are mighty, and they have strong opinions on everything. Plus, they've now been to a few birthday parties, and they know all the goodies they're entitled to and the games they can refuse to play. There is nothing like the horror of standing in the middle of a roomful of four-year-olds all hyped up on birthday cake icing and ice cream, every single one of them screaming and popping balloons while a Responsible Adult (possibly you) tries to get them to play Pin the Tail on the Donkey or something equally uninteresting to them. "How did this ever get started in our culture?" you will cry. "By what insane social convention do I have to put myself through this?"

But you needn't even ask. You still have to do it. And it's not like the first, second, and third birthdays either, when you can invite a bunch of little children over, knowing that their parents or handlers will stay close beside them, and keep them from falling down the stairs, punching out the birthday child, or leaping headfirst into the birthday cake. Your job in those parties is merely to make sure every-one gets something to eat and that your own child does not hurt herself in any kind of permanent way—basically the same tasks you have every other day of your life.

But now the whole new world is dawning, a world in which no other parent will want to stay with you and the children. They will be almost gleeful, in fact, as they drop their little darling child off at the party—speeding away to the beach in their red Corvettes with the top down, shouting over their shoulders, "See ya later! Hope it all goes well!"

Or at least that's how it will feel. I once threw what was to be a ninety-minute birthday party in which every parent dropping off a guest said something like, "Oh, I'm going to be getting a perm this afternoon while Jeffrey is here, so I'm not really sure what time I'll be able to get back here. . . . That's okay, isn't it?" Another said—I'm almost sure she did: "I'll just be having lunch in Paris, but I'm sure the service will be very quick, and I'll get the first flight back that I can. You won't mind keeping Joey if I'm a teensy bit late, will you?"

My hour-and-a-half-and-not-one-minute-longer party turned into a catastrophe. For one thing, none of the guests were hungry for the twenty-four hot dogs I had hoped would take up about twenty minutes of the festivities (more if any food fights broke out). Also, I had figured that opening presents could take another half hour, eating cake and ice cream could be stretched to take at least that much time, and then we'd only have ten minutes to hand out party favors, find everybody's shoes, clean the chocolate cake out of their hair, and wait for their parents to come pick them up. It had seemed that morning to be an extremely workable day.

But seven minutes into the proceedings, I discovered our timetable wasn't going to work. By then all the presents had been opened and discarded, the cake and ice cream had been smeared into the couch cushions, and three people had already boycotted Pin the Tail on the Donkey due to a fear of blindfolds. To entertain themselves, two boys were walking along the back of the sofa, and another was trying to force our cat to wear his winter boots. A fourth child was asking if he could make a fire in the fireplace, and a fifth was throwing up something on the carpeting. All the others were wrestling on the floor under the coffee table—except for a few who had escaped upstairs.

"Put a call in to Paris," I told my husband, "and say that

all flights have to be held until we find Joey's parents. Then call every beauty shop in the city and tell them to refuse a perm to Jeffrey's mom. Then we've got to rope off areas of the house, confine the prisoners to one room, and maybe tie them up until their parents get here."

I have never given what you could call a successful birthday party. Even if I plan for days and hire outside professionals (your various clowns and pony people) to come and entertain, everything seems to go wrong. The clown who shows up turns out to be the scariest individual on the planet, and everyone hides behind the sofa, sniffling, until he promises to take his money and just get the hell out. Kids turn out to be allergic to my potato salad, the hot dogs fall through the grating into the fire on the grill, and my child lapses into a tantrum and starts flinging his gifts at the givers' heads until we subdue him and send him to wait out the rest of the party in his room.

Worse, I've been told that my party favors are the *worst* party favors ever given out. Once, a four-year-old boy accosted me in the kitchen at the end of yet another exhausting, disappointing birthday party. He looked at me sorrowfully and said, "Don't you know that nobody *likes* pig erasers in their party bags? Don't you even know *that?*"

"What do they like?" I asked him, earnestly wanting to know. "What would be good in a party bag?"

"Candy is good," he said. "Not the little boxes of raisins, though. And little trucks and cars. I like elephant erasers, just not pigs, and pencils that have shiny things on them. Girls like little bracelets and rings, but boys don't. Everybody likes chocolate and gum. Some kids like stuff with glitter."

"Do you have a minute so I could get a pencil and piece of paper and take notes?" I asked. "What about games? And should kids get prizes if they win the games, or does that make everything too competitive? What flavors of cake are best? Do kids think it's best to open presents right away, or play for a while first? And how were the hot dogs?"

He considered all this for a few minutes. Then he said, "I don't think I can teach you everything you need to know about parties. Maybe you could get some older kids to come and run things for you. You seem a little nervous."

He was right. After that, I hired twelve-year-olds from the neighborhood to come and run birthday parties. Twelve is just about right; they still remember the good games to play, and they aren't too bossy. Little kids look up to them and will actually even play Kick the Can if a twelve-year-old suggests it.

You pay them five bucks, hover near the sidelines, and life couldn't be better.

Talking about sex

The day will come when your child dispenses with the questions about whether grasshoppers have elbows and turns to the real tough questions of our time. No one is ever prepared for this, so don't worry if you aren't either. Believe me, this isn't the kind of exam you can cram for.

Of course, you're bound to be expecting the "Where did I come from?" question. I don't know anybody who hasn't realized that question is coming and who hasn't been thinking about it since the first labor contraction. I think these days they make you formulate some kind of answer to that even before leaving the hospital. No doubt soon there'll be a checklist to be sure you've got this covered. Right after the question, "Have you purchased a suitable infant car seat?" it will say, "Have you thought about what you'll answer when your child wants to know where s/he came from?"

Let me tell you right now: some kids don't ask. My friend Marge thought she was going to have to bring up the subject herself since her four-year-old didn't seem to be coming up with the necessary curiosity. Marge had bought charts and diagrams and was all ready with the full story of sexual reproduction, but little Emily hadn't come up with a single question about how she'd happened to arrive on the planet.

And then one night, in the middle of the night, there it was. Emily stood by her mother's bed and said, "I want to talk about sex."

Marge flipped on the light, and was just about to retrieve all her flip charts and color-coded materials. "What is it you'd like to know first?" she asked Emily. Maybe she should get the anatomy lessons out of the way first, and then explain about the process of birth, and go on later to the relationship between a man and woman.

"I want to know why ducks don't wear pants," said Emily solemnly.

So Marge put on the brakes, backed up, and entered into a halting explanation of animals' clothing needs— "Some dogs wear sweaters, but mostly animals are fine in their feathers or fur"—and then inquired, rather hopefully, if there wasn't anything else she'd like to know. "Would you like to talk about where babies come from, and how they get born?" she asked.

Emily thought about it for a moment, and then said, "I don't think so," and trotted back to bed.

Some would say that Marge got off easily, but believe me, she was vastly disappointed and also felt guilty in a weird way. Most mothers can work up a case of guilt over just about anything, and Marge was no exception. She kept asking all her friends if there was something untrustworthy about her. "You'd listen to anything I had to say on the subject of sex, wouldn't you?" she said. "I mean, I know *something* about it. I have a child, after all."

We all had to assure her that we were perfectly sure her

sexual know-how was tiptop, and that anytime she wished to explain the facts of reproduction to any of us, we'd be glad to hear her out. Our friend Cheryl observed that perhaps the real reason Emily wasn't asking the tough questions was precisely *because* Marge was so prepared.

"She'll probably ask you something about the theory of relativity instead—something you didn't think to brush up on," said Cheryl.

Naturally, though, in her quest to be what the books all call an "askable parent," Marge went through a tough phase when she followed Emily around, spouting off information on an unasked-for basis.

"Babies come from seeds from both the mother and the father," she'd say at breakfast. And then later, perhaps while they were cleaning up the dinner dishes, "Babies grow inside the mother from a seed that the daddy knows how to plant there."

Such startling facts were lost on Emily, however, who would simply nod and go about her life. Finally Marge stopped with the guerrilla sex education—and then one day, at the age of eight, Emily came to her wanting the full story. She started out with, "Now, *puh-leaze* don't start talking about animals wearing clothes again—but I want to know how people get babies."

Death and the meaning of life

But I have to warn you: there are way tougher questions than "Where did I come from?"

It's usually when a kid is four that she starts to muse on the possibility that not only can't she remember how she arrived on the planet but she's thinking that someday she might have to leave it as well. And she'd like to get your thoughts on this.

"How am I going to die?" you'll be asked.

It is best, if you can manage, *not* to drop your coffee in your lap in your rush to run over and hug her. In fact, it would be terrific all around if you could just calmly say something like, "Well, none of us knows how we're going to die."

The questions after that will vary. *Does everything die? Where do we go when we die? Will I still eat ice cream when I'm dead?* Stuff like that. These are the questions you can't just answer with a flippant reply and go on about your life.

I once spent the better part of twenty minutes answering questions about death. My four-year-old and I ruminated together on just how limited human beings' knowledge of the Great Unknown is; we talked calmly and sanely about how death is just part of life, and therefore we try to live our lives fully every day because we don't know what will happen. We talked about how we *hate* the fact that we can't know what's going to happen and how it's going to be for us, and I went on to detail my philosophy of love and forgiveness, touching briefly on what it meant to be a fragile being and going on anyway.

When I got finished, we sat there in the dark, her head on my shoulder, breathing in the stillness.

Finally she spoke. "But not you and me, right?" she said. "We live forever."

8

Your Life, Interrupted Even More

Take bedtime—please

I have to admit right now that I have never known how to get children to go to bed. So if you are thinking that somewhere in this book there will be the secret of children going to sleep and not disrupting your entire night, I'm afraid I can't help much.

When it comes to bedtime, I do everything the books say: try to make the evening a calm time rather than something resembling the halftime show at the Super Bowl. I speak of bedtime in a longing, quiet voice—almost sepulchral tones, some would say. Then, when it's finally time to take everybody upstairs, I read the stories, sing the lullabies, and say the ritual good-nights.

And nothing happens. The kids go on as usual, acting the same way they acted all evening long. It's as though they didn't even notice.

Five minutes after I've turned the lights out, they are all back on again—and children are wandering the house in search of glasses of water, interesting conversations, and even the late-night movie schedule.

It's always been this way, too. From the first night home from the hospital, not one of my three children has ever fallen asleep willingly. When they were babies, friends would come over at bedtime to bestow their advice and wisdom on me and point out any mistakes I might have unwittingly been making. For instance, it was possible, I suppose, that when I said, "Time to go to sleep now," my children were misinterpreting this to mean, "Time to jump on the beds and have a good time." You never know, I suppose, when you could be communicating a mixed message.

But time after time, I'd do the bedtime ritual, and my friend/observer of the evening would smile approvingly, and say, "Now this is the point where *my* children nod off to sleep. I'm sure yours will be out like lights in just a few moments."

Not mine. Within moments, they'd be doing fan dances and wanting to discuss draft picks in the NFL, the causes of the Civil War, and the world's banking plan for the next decade. Anything to keep from shutting their eyes and drifting off to a pleasant oblivion.

Here's an example of a bedtime story hour with my youngest child when she was four, just to let you know how bad things could get:

"Once upon a time," I said, "there was a little girl named Goldilocks."

Just so you know, I was telling this story out of my own memory. I had already read her the required two stories from a book and had sung her two songs, and now to fulfill the terms of my obligation, I had to *tell* her a story, and then I was to be allowed to leave the room, and she was legally required to close her eyes.

"One day she was walking—"

"Why is her name Goldilocks?"

"Because she had golden hair. *Anyway*, she was walking in the forest one morning, and she got lost."

"She got *lost* in the forest? Where was her mother?"

"Back at home."

"How old is she?"

"Uh, eight."

"When I'm eight, am I going to be allowed to walk in the forest by myself?"

"No, you're not. But *she* was walking in the forest, and she came to a little house that three bears lived in. The bears had gone for a walk because their porridge was too hot, and—"

"Wait a minute! Bears live in a *house?*"

"In this story, bears live in a house. In real life, bears just live in the woods. Anyway, their porridge was too hot, so—"

"What is porridge?"

"Porridge is like oatmeal, and it was too hot, so they went for a walk."

"When my oatmeal is too hot, I just blow on it. I don't go for a walk."

"While the bears were gone, Goldilocks saw their little house, and she decided to go inside."

"*What?* Didn't she knock first?"

"She did knock, but when no one answered, she went in."

"Why didn't the bears lock their door?"

"Maybe they were just going to be gone a few minutes, and they weren't expecting anyone out in the forest, so they didn't lock it."

"Maybe that's why they call her Goldilocks. It's not because her hair is gold. It's because she goes in doors that aren't locked."

"Could be. First she saw the porridge and she decided to taste it. She took a bite of Papa Bear's porridge and it was *too hot.* Then she tasted Mama Bear's porridge and it was *too cold.* Then she tasted Baby Bear's porridge, and it was *just right.* So she ate it all up."

"How could one bowl be too hot when the other bowl was already too cold?"

"I don't really know. *Then* she went into the living room, and she saw the bears' chairs. She sat in Papa Bear's chair and it was *too hard.* So she sat in Mama Bear's chair and it was *too soft.* Baby Bear's chair was *just right,* but when she sat in it, it broke."

"I think there's going to be trouble."

"She went upstairs, and there she saw the bears' beds. First she tried Papa Bear's bed, but it was *too hard,* so she tried Mama Bear's bed, and it was *too soft.*"

"Why does Papa Bear have everything so hard?"

"Maybe he likes it that way."

"He should get a new chair and bed. But I guess they need to spend the money on Baby Bear's chair, now that Goldilocks broke it."

"So Goldilocks tried Baby Bear's bed, and it was *just right.* So she got in it and fell asleep."

"Did it break, too?"

"No. But then the bears came home."

She hid her eyes.

"Papa Bear walked into the kitchen and said, 'Somebody's been eating my porridge!' "

"Oh, no! How could he tell? She didn't eat it all up; she just tasted it!"

"Maybe she left the spoon in it. Anyway, Mama Bear said somebody had been tasting her porridge, too, and Baby Bear said, 'And somebody's been tasting my porridge, and they ate it all up!' "

"The bears will have to make him some more."

"Then they went into the living room, and Papa Bear and Mama Bear both said, 'Somebody's been sitting in our chairs!' "

"Now, wait a minute! They couldn't tell *that.* You don't know if somebody was sitting in a chair."

"Well, these bears were very sensitive. They knew lots of things. And then Baby Bear showed them that his chair was broken apart."

"Was he crying?"

"Yes. Yes, he was. And they went upstairs, and Papa Bear said, 'Somebody's been sleeping in my bed!' "

"Well, he's wrong about *that*. She never slept in his bed. She just *tried* it."

"That's right. Anyway, Mama Bear said somebody had been *trying* her bed, too, and then Baby Bear said, 'Somebody's been sleeping in my bed, too, and there she is right now!' "

"Was he still mad about the chair?"

"I think he was just surprised. But nobody was more surprised than Goldilocks when she woke up and saw the three bears staring at her. She got so scared she ran out of their house and never came back again."

"She didn't even say she was sorry for all the trouble she made?"

"She was too scared. Those were three mad bears."

"She probably didn't expect bears to be living in a house."

"Probably not."

"But I don't think that's a very nice story anyway. I think her name is weird and she was a bad girl to do that stuff and make Baby Bear cry. And I think you need to tell me another story because that one doesn't count."

A look around at your life

Every now and then, I think, it's useful to take stock. You need to take a look around at your own life and get a measure of how much it has changed now that you are living with a person who asks an average of 437 questions a day.

Take your ears, for instance. Sometimes, by the time my own bedtime arrived, I had to go and stare at my ears in the mirror just to see if they were red and throbbing from all the talking they'd endured that day. There were nights I was sure they must be bleeding—or at least would have bloomed into something resembling cauliflowers just from overuse.

But no. Looking in the mirror, night after night, all I'd see would be a rather bleary-eyed face looking back at me, eyes unfocused and disengaged—but, near as I could tell, the ears were still connected to the sides of the head and with no noticeable scabs, even. Ears can take a lot of damage and still remain intact.

Once you've ascertained that your ears are still on your head, one on each side, it's a good idea to stroll through the house and measure your environment now against what it used to be. How far have you come? Or, as my friend Lillie put it: how much does your house look like all those people's houses you swore you'd never live like, back before you had children?

It happens, you know, when you're not even looking.

The bathroom: The tub has rubber duckies stacked up in the corners; the walls have been written on with special bath crayons that are supposed to rinse off (and probably will sometime in the next two years if somebody ever gets around to it, and if the stuff doesn't have a half-life equal to nuclear waste); there are three red plastic boats; some pink foam things stuck to the wall and to the bottom of the tub; two kinds of tearless baby shampoo and bottles of kid conditioner and kid body wash sitting on the counter. In front of the sink is a little wooden stool, useful for people under three feet tall who need to reach the toothbrushes. You have stubbed your toe on it every night for two years, and even now your toe is throbbing in anticipation of hitting it once more.

The kitchen: Alphabet magnets on the refrigerator spell

"MOM HELP." (You're pretty sure that *you* wrote that.) There are plastic cereal bowls with the Teletubbies' pictures on them stacked up on the countertop. Three Lego pieces from a spaceship are on the floor, one dangerously close to making it under the refrigerator. Your hairbrush is on top of the toaster, along with Barbie's tutu, the axle of a truck, and the cap to a tippy cup. A blue dinosaur is sitting in the roasting pan on the floor. Floating in a puddle of spilled orange juice on the counter is a notice from the nursery school, which claims that you are responsible for bringing snacks next week and that you must attend a Parent Cleanup Day on Saturday. Someone has scrawled in: "Bring steel wool to clean the hardened Play-Doh off the riding toys. Also, re: snack! *No more* store-bought cupcakes. Yuck!!!! We want HEALTHY SNACKS for our kids!!" (You stop a moment to wonder if *everyone* knows it was you, or could you get away with pretending outrage along with the rest of them?)

On the windowsill, there's a bottle of Baby Tylenol drops, along with Robitussin DM and a bottle of Flintstones multivitamins, with all the Dinos eaten out of it.

Next to these are bottles of Stress-relief tabs, super-stress B-complex vitamins, and gingko biloba.

Otherwise known as your lifelines.

Your bedroom: Now, here's where it's possible to get a little nostalgic for what used to be. Your bed is unmade, for the seventh day straight, and next to your pillow is a yellow Tonka truck (you remember hitting your head against something metal all night long, but it wasn't until now that you can see what it is). Your husband's pillow is on the floor and has a wet spot in the middle of it, a wet spot you don't want to think about but have to because there's a knocked-over tippy cup nearby. What was in it—milk? juice? water from the toilet? There is no telling. In your dirty clothes basket there's a Tigger doll poking his head up over the stacks of dirty laundry. There's a wet towel lying across the comforter on the bed. On the dresser, your tubes of lipstick are all open, and all broken off. A bead necklace has come apart, spilling red and blue beads all over the dresser. (You've promised to fix that sometime, but many of the beads went into the heater vent, and you haven't wanted to face the fact with your child that once you string it together, it's going to be more a toe ring than a necklace.) The lampshade is askew and has a pair of size-three tiger-striped pajama pants hanging from it; two Barbie dolls are using your husband's dirty socks for sleeping bags; and the M–Z section of an Italian-English dictionary is riding in a Fisher Price airplane, which a red-haired, round-bottomed Weeble is piloting into your closet.

Your child's room: Don't go in. Why break your own heart?

Who knew that notepads are the answer to getting kids to mind?

If they ever give classes in Managing Little Children (and I really think this is something that psychiatrists and pediatricians might want to look into), there should be a whole classroom period devoted to the science and philosophy of notepads.

It turns out that even little kids know that the written word is a powerful tool, and you can get them to accept almost anything simply by writing it down and reading it to them. This is a little-known secret in the world of parent-child relations, and I don't think it's been publicized enough as a parenting tool. As far as I know, there haven't even been any studies to discover just why it works.

But you don't need to know how it works. You just need

to get your kid to put on his shoes so you can take him to the dentist.

You say, "Let's get your shoes on so we can go to the dentist."

He says, "I don't want to put on my shoes."

You whip out your notepad and write that down. "Jack does not want to put on his shoes." You read it back to him.

Then—here's the unbelievable part—Jack beams at you and puts on his shoes.

So then you say, "Now that you have your shoes on, let's go get in the car and go to the dentist."

"But I hate going to the dentist! I don't want to go!"

Another note. "Jack hates going to the dentist. He does not want to go." You give him this note to hold in his car seat. At first you might expect that a kid would probably eat the note on the way, just because—well, who wouldn't think of eating a perfectly good piece of note paper whenever the opportunity presented itself? But no. Later you realize that Jack wouldn't dream of eating the note because of its *officialness*. You eat a note like that, and then you don't have your documentation anymore. Even Jack knows that.

I once succeeded in getting a four-year-old to walk the five blocks home from nursery school simply through a system of note writing. It took a while—I won't deny that. You could find me stalled on one street corner after another, scrawling little notes and handing them over to my child. They said things like: "Stephanie does not want to walk to the next streetlight." And then we'd walk to the next streetlight, and she'd say, "Now I don't want to walk to the stop sign." And so there'd be another note, and so on and so on until we made it all the way to the front door.

Okay, so it's crazy. It was better than arguing and pleading. Or worse, carrying.

I should warn you, though, there did come a day when

the Notepad System backfired. We had left the nursery school in a huge hurry, and we were about halfway home when Stephanie realized she had brought with her a book she was writing and illustrating, called *The Little Girl Who Met the Ballerina and Saw Her Necklace Fall Off on the Floor.* It was a moving story of a blue-haired little girl with talonlike fingers who one day met a yellow-haired ballerina in a pink tutu, and then there was some situation about a necklace and the suspicion of thievery.

And there we were carrying this book *away* from the nursery school where it belonged.

Immediately she was in full-scale hysteria. "This book was supposed to stay at school for me to finish tomorrow! Now I'll never remember to take it back, and I won't get to finish it. We've got to take it back right now! Take it back! Turn around!"

I did not want to go back. For one thing, it was a cold day and we'd already walked nearly three blocks, and for another thing, I had to get home for an important phone call. But here's the thing: the old me would have suggested she finish the book at home, which of course is an idiotic suggestion because books can only be finished in the spot where they were begun; any writer knows that.

Instead, I whipped out a notepad and explained how we could write a note to help us remember to take it back the next day. I started writing: "Bring back the—"

"I want to write the note!" she roared. "Give me the paper!"

I handed it over with a sigh and started spelling, "B . . . R . . ."

"No, that's not the way I want to say it," she said. She lay down on the sidewalk on her stomach and stared off into the distance, thinking hard. "Spell this for me: Dear Mommy, Stephanie did not mean to bring home her book, named *The Little Girl Who Met the Ballerina and Saw Her Neck-*

lace Fall Off on the Floor. That book has to go back to the nursery school in the morning because Stephanie didn't finish writing the story and drawing the pictures and the teachers at her school would like to see it when it is finished. This book must go back. Love, Stephanie."

She looked up at me and smiled. "Does 'Dear' start with a D?"

Why we can't be on vacation when we're still in the driveway

At some point, in spite of the fact that you are the parent of a little child, you will decide that you should take a vacation. No, no, not just a fun vacation from work and home—this will be a *family vacation.*

This will seem like a wonderful idea at first. You start to notice that lots of people take their kids on vacation. Suddenly, as never before, the roads seem filled with cars that have suitcases piled on the top and children peering out of the back windows. You see ads for Family Vacation Packages on every page of the newspaper. There are even books in the library and magazine articles, promising to tell you How to Survive a Family Vacation with Anyone Younger Than the Age of Rationality (which, I believe, is now hovering around twenty-four these days.) There will be a smiling woman in the photo, holding on to three children who may or may not have had lobotomies. You'll have a moment's pause at the word "survive" in the title—but then you realize the article has lots of important tips for you, things like, "Don't leave your child in any public restrooms along the route" and "Find games to play in the car so that the time goes by faster."

Of course, your children will have plenty of ideas about games to play in the car. The favorite one, of course, is Kick the Front Seat. The great thing about this game is that it's just as much fun for only one person as it is for many players, and it can go on for hours and hours without any discernible letup. Also, it has its own script.

After approximately ten minutes of steady, thrumming kicks against the back of your seat, you will remember that your valuable kidneys are located near the Impact Zone, and, fearing a lifetime of dialysis, you will say, "Honey, please stop kicking the back of my seat."

"Okay," the child will say. And up to three minutes in some cases have gone by before the kicking resumes—at first, light, delicate kicks but soon turning into genuine blows.

You: "I said to please stop kicking the back of my seat."
The Kid: "I did stop."
You: "But then you started again."
The Kid: "But I *did* stop."
You: "Yes, that's right. You did stop. But now you are kicking my seat once again, and I would like you to stop."
The Kid: "Can I just do four more kicks?"
You: "No, you can't do four more kicks. I want you to stop it *now*."
The Kid: (still kicking) "What about six more kicks?"
You: "Am I going to have to pull this car over and *make* you stop kicking my seat?"
The Kid: "I'm not kicking you. My foot is doing it, and my foot doesn't have ears so he doesn't know you want him to stop."
You: "You'd better tell your foot right this minute, or I'm going to tell your foot myself! And it won't be pretty!"
The Kid: "Fine! But it is a bad foot, so it probably won't listen."
You: (beginning to feel the first stages of kidney failure) "I know how to make a foot listen. If I have to pull over and

talk to that foot myself, *then* it will understand why it shouldn't kick people's seats anymore!"

You drive along in peace for a short while, marveling at a life that can bring a rational human being to make such a statement as "I know how to make a foot listen." Ten years ago, if someone had told you that you'd be one day threatening to pull your car over to the side of the road and make a foot listen, would you have decided the world had gone mad? Well, the truth is, when you're the parent of someone tiny *and* you're on a family vacation, the world will seem to have gone mad quite a few times.

There's another popular Car Game, one you might remember from your own childhood. It's the Are We There Yet game, and the best part of this game, from a child's point of view, is that all she has to do is murmur it every few minutes or so, and soon you will be a blithering idiot, babbling and furious, practically foaming at the mouth. There's hardly any better entertainment than that on a long, monotonous drive.

We were once driving from Connecticut to Cape Cod and had gotten only to the base of our driveway when our four-year-old asked that the first time.

I pulled over. "Did you just ask if we were there yet?"

"Yes," she said.

"Do you still see our house?"

"Yes."

"Well, how could we be in Cape Cod if we can still see our house? How could that be?"

Silence.

"Our house isn't in Cape Cod," I said, "so if we see our house, then we must still be at home."

There was a long silence while she looked out the window. Then she said, "I thought maybe there would be a house like ours at Cape Cod."

"No," I said. "There isn't."

"You don't know for sure! Maybe there's a house just like our house and other people live in it, and when they come to Connecticut, their kid says, 'Are we there yet?' And that mommy says, 'Why are you saying that already?' "

"I'm glad," I said finally, "that we're having this little talk right now, because I don't want to travel three hundred fifty miles with you asking me every few minutes if we're there yet. We can take care of this right now. We won't be there for four hours. Four hours. That's like watching Barney eight times. Eight Barneys."

"Barney only comes on two times."

"Right. So you can see that it will be a very long time, and you should look out the window at the trees and the clouds instead of thinking we're there already."

We rode down the street for three more nanoseconds.

"Mommy."

"Yes?"

"Can I ask you a question?"

"Okay."

"Is it almost time to ask if we're there yet?"

The vacation question derby

One thing about vacationing with children—especially those who are preschoolers—is that whole new areas of questions are opened up. When you remain at home all the time, you see, the same territory gets mined again and again for all possible knowledge, and eventually (this takes years) the questions all get asked and answered. But take your little family show out on the road, and there's no end to the new questions that have to be asked.

Four-year-olds need to know *everything*. It's as though they think they're about to be given responsibility for the entire world, and they want to make sure they've got all the details straight before they take over. They're understandably worried about getting something wrong, and having the whole world come crashing to an end.

The year we went to Cape Cod with our four-year-old, she was stunned to realize that we were planning to live for a week in a different house.

"But it has furniture in it already!" she said.

"Yes, isn't that great?" I said.

"Who put the furniture here?"

"The people who own it."

"But where are they? Why are they letting us take their house away? And why did they pick these couches and not different ones? What if they come back while we're here? Why did they put forks and spoons in that drawer and not this drawer? What plates are they eating on if we have their plates? Is somebody staying in our house while we're not there? *Is some other kid sleeping in my bed like I'm sleeping in this kid's bed?*"

After I'd explained the cottage rental system to her satisfaction, we went on to discuss people who buy campers. As luck would have it, we had passed one in the car.

"Is that a house or a car?" she wanted to know. "Why do people want to sleep in their car instead of taking someone else's house away from them? Is it because they're afraid the people will come back and want their house while they're there? Where is the driving wheel of that thing? Can you take a bath and drive at the same time? Do people who have campers sleep in real houses, too?"

Just the first day alone, I'd told her everything I knew about campers, but over the next few days we had to discuss tents, lighthouses, the origins of bath towels, and how lobsters get rubber bands on their claws. Then we were onto how potato chips get in the bags, where Popsicle sticks come from, why baby bunnies live at the miniature golf place, why cars use gas, and—my favorite—how many green highway signs there are in the world.

"I don't know," I gasped. My brain was hurting. Twenty-four hours on vacation, and I was wishing I could go back to work.

She was leaning over the front seat of the car, two inches from my face. "Could you take a guess, please?" she whispered sweetly.

"Four billion—about the same number of questions you have," I told her.

"Can I ask you one more question?"

"Yes."

"When can I ask you if we're almost home yet?"

The true story of baby-sitters

Sometimes, vacation or no vacation, you realize that you need to get out of the house. By this I mean: out among adults. I don't have to tell you why. The symptoms are clear. Maybe you can't get the Barney theme song out of your head. Perhaps you have red Play-Doh clinging to your clothing. Or worse, just the other day you may have seen a couple walking down the street, hand in hand, and you thought, "Oh, my God! They're going to be so upset when they realize they forgot their *child* somewhere! I should alert them that the kid is missing!" You were just about to roll down your car window and shout to them when you remembered that not *every couple* has a little child swinging between them when they walk anywhere.

Some people get to go out in public alone. And you see that you had better wash the Play-Doh off and go join them soon.

Be prepared, though. This one evening out will take more planning than many two-week vacations you took when you were single. For one thing, you will have to find a baby-sitter. This usually means that you have to call up every teenager you and your friends have ever heard of, and beg each of them in turn to come to your house for a few hours. This is going to take hours, and no doubt you'll be hoarse and discouraged at the end of it.

Teenagers, you will discover, don't want to come take care of our children because they are living fabulous, fun lives, which they will very tactlessly tell you about. "Oh, I can't do that," one will say, "because I'm like going to the Stones concert that night."

It's no good to ask how a *thirteen-year-old* gets to see the Stones when there are many full-fledged *adults* who do not have tickets, even though these adults legitimately grew *up* with the Stones' music and have waited in long lines to get tickets in the past, and who even now would give anything to get tickets, but can't because they didn't even *hear* about the concert because they have to play the *Sesame Street* tape in the car and never get to listen to rock on the radio anymore.

So, after composing yourself and stifling a small sob, you say, "Well . . . how about the *next* weekend?"

"Ohhh, that's like the weekend we're heading like to Vermont to ski."

"Wow! Well! Anything open the . . . *next* weekend?"

"Hmmm. I would, but that's the day after Brittany is having her sleep-over, and I'll probably be like waaay too tired."

"Listen, kid, you do know I plan to *pay* you for this," you hear yourself growling. "Don't teenagers need spending money anymore?"

"Like how much were you planning to pay?" she asks.

"Fifty billion dollars. I'll give you fifty billion dollars if you will come to my house and watch my kid so I can go out to dinner!"

"Um, I think I'd rather see the Stones."

We have succeeded occasionally in getting a teenager to come to our house. I don't know how we did it. Money, jewels, promises of concert tickets—I can't remember. Actually, the truth is that sometimes you run into a kid who needs to recharge her bank account temporarily, and if you promise to stock the house with M&Ms, potato chips, and ice-cold sodas, sometimes a kid in a temporary Life Slump will agree to baby-sit for you. This, I don't have to warn you, will cost at least as much as the dinner out— and may have hidden costs, such as an astronomical phone bill later that month. (Sometimes baby-sitters, understandably, feel they need to consult with the Psychic Network while they're at your home, but don't worry: no doubt they are asking advice on how to better care for your child.)

It helps in luring a baby-sitter to your home if you can boast that you've loaded up on several items in advance. We've found it helpful to advertise that we have the following on hand:

- Several gallons of her favorite soda, in addition to the above-mentioned snack foods (If she's a first-time sitter, you might want to inquire about any food preferences, allergies, complexion problems, etc.)
- At least five flavors of ice cream
- Two telephone lines
- An Internet connection, complete with open chat rooms
- Premium cable access
- The latest issues of all the hot teen magazines

- Spare cash on hand for any pizza deliveries that may be required
- The promise of much more cash at the end of the evening (It's best to be vague about the exact amount, or she may start a bidding war among your so-called friends.)

Sick days—and nights

There's nothing that can prepare you for how your life lurches into disarray when your child is sick. Sick kids are the most pathetic and scary things on earth. When they're babies, of course, it's terrible to see them sick because you go out of your mind from fright. After all, they can't talk and they look pitiful, with those bright red blotchy cheeks and the runny nose and filmy eyes. You're running around, half-wild with fear, dosing them with Tylenol and antibiotics, with calls in to the doctor every few hours, and deep down, even if it's only a cold they're sick with, you're thinking, "Just don't die. *Please don't die!*"

Somehow, though, bad as infant illness is, it's worse when they get older and can talk. Then you really *know* how awful they feel, because they're explaining it to you in excruciating detail, day in and day out.

A sick baby will snuggle up in your lap and sleep on you for hours, burning a feverish hole into your midsection. But sick kids don't sleep. They can't, because who will tell you all their troubles if they're sound asleep? They need to stay awake so they can keep you apprised of all health bulletins as they become available.

A sick kid will come into your room in the middle of the night to tell you his Top 30 symptoms. Among them are: head aches, stomach hurts, nose is running, throat is sore, chest feels tight, eyebrows are stuck in the up position.

It's the flu, of course. What else strikes both the throat *and* eyebrows with such vengeance?

You get up on one elbow, and say, "It sounds like you're sick. The best thing to do is to go back to bed and get as much healing sleep as you possibly can."

He looks doubtful at this, so you take him in and tuck him back in, give him some Tylenol and a drink of water, which he says tastes as yucky as dog poop, and then you go back to bed. Twenty minutes later, though, he's noticed something new, which is that his eyeballs are boiling, so he comes to tell you about it.

"You need sleep," you say blearily. "Your eyeballs are not boiling. You just have the flu. Now go back to sleep."

"Also my hairs are hurting, and I think some of them are sticking into my brains inside."

"It's the flu."

"And my knees are bumping."

You walk him back into his room and tuck him in again.

"I think you should sleep here with me because one of my ears is going boom boom boom," he says.

"Your ears are fine, don't worry."

"I think they're bleeding."

"They're not bleeding."

"I think you need to sleep in my bed to make sure I don't get sicker."

"Okay, what if I stay here just until you fall asleep and then I'll go back to my own bed?"

"My throat itches and my eyes are burning."

"I know. Try to sleep."

Ha! There is no sleep to be had. Soon toenails are throbbing, the little bit of skin right near his earlobe has developed a nasty new crease, and hairs are *definitely* being sucked back up into the head by the brains. You fetch drinks of water, tell stories about why you shouldn't have chosen to write your thesis in college on the Italian Renaissance (nobody has ever been willing to listen to this diatribe before), and pat his damp little forehead until—just as the sun comes up—the *two* of you fall asleep.

When you wake up hours later, your neck has been dislocated from the rest of your spine from sleeping in an area one-sixteenth of a single bed, and it's just possible that your brains are sucking some of the hairs back into your body and that your eyeballs are boiling. You stagger in to get some Tylenol and a drink of water, and when you get back, your child is sitting on the side of his bed, vomiting into his only pair of sneakers.

I don't have the heart to tell you about the *next* three days.

The return to health

My friend Hallie says that it's always 2:00 A.M. when kids get sick, and it's always 4:00 A.M. several eons later when they get well. There's no good reason for this, but that's the way it happens. You'll put a kid to bed when he's feeling medium rotten on Night Five of the flu, and then at 4:00 A.M., you'll hear a sprightly knock at your bedroom door, and a voice saying, "Yoo-hoo! Time to get up! It snowed last night, and I think we should have some pancakes and orange juice and then go outside sledding! I've been downstairs and I found everybody's mittens and hats."

You poke your husband, and whisper, "Who do you think that is at our bedroom door?"

He has no idea.

But, just as you feared, it's your kid, all right. Sometime between the dead of night and the middle of the night he's found his way back to the bloom of health, and he's ready to make up for lost time. Even, apparently, the lost time that took place before he was born.

You're glad, of course, that he's well. In fact, you feel waves of relief coming over you. There won't be trips to the hospital, in which a kindly doctor explains that if you'd just thought to bring your child in to be examined back months ago when the fever first *started,* then maybe he'd have some-day walked again. There won't be years of rehabilitation in sanitariums, special schools, whole-body braces. It *was* just the flu, after all.

But there he is, calling you through the door at 4:04 A.M.

"Maybe after we go sledding, we could go to the video store and get some videos about Star Wars," he says. "I want to play Luke Skywalker today, and I forgot what his costume looks like. Then we could get hot dogs with mustard—"

"Hot dogs with mustard! It's four in the morning!"

"But I'm *hungry!*"

"I think you're still sick."

"No, I want to *eat.* I want to play. Do you think I could call Mark up? Is it a school day or a home day? Is the sled in the garage or in the shed? I'm going outside to see!"

You get up. It's a school day. You make pancakes for breakfast (he eats nine of them) and pack his lunch. You find the sleds in the garage and take a sled ride with him in the backyard before it's time for him to leave. He's got bright eyes and no fever. You grab him for a hug as he runs past you, up the slope for one last ride.

As you're packing him in the car to go to nursery school with Daddy, he says to you, "Would you just do one thing for me? Would you pretend you're chasing the car all the way to the corner when we drive away?"

And you know something? You're so glad he's well, and so filled with gratitude and relief—and okay, pancakes—

that you do it. Being careful not to slip on the snow, you pretend to run to the corner with the car. And in the backseat, you can see his laughing face, hysterical to watch you doing this for him.

He's well, you think, as the car turns the corner one more time.

9

Signs You Live with a Preschooler

- You don't know where your curling iron is, but last time it was lost you found it in the dryer, dressed in Barbie's wedding dress.
- It's 7:25 A.M., and you have already answered 326 questions concerning such topics as how stomachs turn Cheerios into poops, the whereabouts of bees during the winter, the reason that television programs can't just come through the walls but have to be on TV screens, and the reason that the words "aunt" and "ant" sound alike.
- There are two tricycles, a riding toy, a plastic lawnmower, a Fisher Price life-size house, and fourteen facedown baby dolls out in the rain in your front yard.
- Your couch cushions smell like rancid apple juice.
- The telephone receiver is so sticky you can't hang up the phone once you've answered it.
- A toy fire truck is sitting in the middle of the kitchen missing one wheel, and your child says the dog ate it.

- The dog is also said to be responsible for the red Magic Marker picture on the family room wall.
- There's a green Lego sticking out of the top of the toaster. Your child says it's a waffle for the plastic firefighters who are waiting for the dog to throw up the wheel to the fire truck so they can get back to work.
- The magnetic alphabet letters on the refrigerator spell a dirty word, which your child insists he invented.
- The dog is gagging uncontrollably.
- There are three melted crayons in the windowsill.
- A baby stroller blocking the doorway contains the following items: your pay stub from last month, a half-full bag of cat litter, a knitting needle, an extension cord, the knobs to the dresser drawers in your child's room, the purse you carried last New Year's Eve, three action figures from McDonald's last promotion, a piece of pink chalk, your high school diploma, an hors d'oeuvre fork, a red bow from last Christmas.
- Your child says there may be a lizard loose in the bathroom, and he could be right.
- You've had a song called "Punchinello" going through your head for the last three weeks, and you realize it's from a video that plays continuously at your house.
- The baby-sitter says she can't find her car keys since your child borrowed them.
- Your child says it was the firefighters who borrowed them because they couldn't get their own fire truck to work since the wheel, etc., etc.
- After a three-person, one-hour search, the car keys are located in the bushes in the front yard,

along with a ruler, a five-inch ladder, and a plate
of plastic spaghetti.

- Your child says the neighbors must have come
  over in the night and done that.
- You have three Barbie high heels in your suit
  pocket.
- You have eaten macaroni and cheese every night
  for six weeks.
- Your child is wearing a pair of Wonder Woman
  underwear, a tiara, and a pair of winter boots
  while she eats her breakfast.
- The last time you went to the gas station, the at-
  tendant found a Weeble in the gas tank compartment.
- The three lipsticks you bought last week all have
  only one-quarter inch of stuff left in them.
- Your child's nursery school teacher told you that
  your child has "lots of creative energy and an as-
  sertive playground demeanor" and your best
  friend has informed you this was not a compli-
  ment.
- Your VCR won't work, and the repairman said
  he's never seen so much mayonnaise in an elec-
  trical appliance.
- Every night in the middle of the night, your child
  comes and asks if he can sleep in your bed with
  you twenty minutes earlier than he did the night
  before. By the end of the week, you figure he'll
  be there before you even get there.
- Just the other day he asked you, "When I was a
  child, were you young?"

10

Life Among the Toys

Lose the rubber chicken while you still have your brain intact

Okay, so you were looking forward to the toys.

In fact, for a lot of people who aren't so certain they'd be good Parent Material—and who can ever be *truly* sure?—the toys are one of the deciding factors to go ahead and reproduce yourself. You figure that even if you can't do great at teaching classical music and explaining Western philosophy to your kid, at least you're relatively sure you can get down on the floor and build an airplane out of Legos. Besides, you think to yourself, it might be fun to play with all those cool Tinkertoys and Lincoln logs again. And damn it, you were *great* at Legos. And model airplanes. And even the baby dolls they show on television these days look so interesting—the way they not only eat, wet, and ride on roller skates but some of them even have pregnancy pouches and produce another little baby doll at some point.

I'm afraid I have a warning for you: Be careful when you're buying toys for your child. Like so much else in the modern age, the toys aren't all they seem on the surface, and you can find yourself living a hideous existence, inundated with toys who are taking over your entire reality.

For instance, for what seemed like several eons but what was probably only two thousand years at the most, we lived in the Diner from Hell. We had made the mistake of buying our daughter a set of realistic-looking plastic food, dishes, silverware, and the kind of ketchup and mustard squeeze bottles only found in diners with at least three calendars hanging on the wall. The box these devices came in promised that this would "stimulate your child's imagination to the utmost," which we did not see as the warning it was surely meant to be. Looking back months later, my husband said, "Why did they have to add that 'to the utmost' phrase anyway? We just wanted to stimulate her imagination, period. Not to the utmost. *Certainly* not to the utmost."

That's the kind of thing you don't notice when you're intent on buying a kid an imaginative present. What we failed to take into consideration was that this was a child who was already so steeped in the world of fantasy that often it was difficult to make contact with her. But as soon as she had put on the waitress hairnet and the apron and had grabbed onto the notepad, our days of living sanely alongside her were over for good.

It didn't matter what else you might be doing—sleeping, taking a bath, backing down the driveway in the car—there she'd be, pencil shoved behind the ear, and saying in a Brooklyn accent, "Hon, what you like?"

Here are the responses that *didn't* work for us. Maybe you would have more luck with your own child:

- "Nothing now, honey. I'm in the middle of negotiating a merger between two major oil companies, so I'm a little bit busy."
- "I ate a huge lunch today, so I'm not hungry."
- "I really don't have a taste for plastic peas today, thanks."

Nope. Whenever our waitress was in the mood to serve up some plastic food, we had better be in the mood to eat some of it, or else she followed us around the house, putting it in front of us at every opportunity and calling us "hon."

She'd say, "Hon, you need to eat. You get grouchy when you're hungry."

"All right," I'd say.

"What you like, hon?"

"I'll have the spaghetti and bread."

"We're out of that, hon."

"Okay, the chicken leg and the peas."

"Outta that too, hon."

"All *right,* then. The cheese Danish."

"Oh, hon, we don't got that."

"Then. Give. Me. The. Plastic. Scrambled. Egg."

At this point she would sigh and shake her hair out of the hairnet. "Mom! The scrambled egg is *not* plastic," she said. "You have to pretend this is real."

"Well," I said. "If we're pretending this is real, then I happen to know you have all those foods I asked for. But you say you're out of them so that I have to think harder and play the game longer."

She smiled. "That's good, to play the game a long time."

"Fine," I said. "Then give me the pizza."

"Oh, no!" she said. "Somebody else just ordered the last pizza we have. I think you should come sit down at the table with the tablecloth and look at the menu. Then you'll be happy."

Barbie and her lifestyle

For years, I fought against Barbie. Like many women I know, I felt that Barbie didn't set a good example for children because she was insipid and had too many clothes—and besides that, I frankly resented the monster-size ta-tas and that one-inch waist she flaunts. I felt these proportions were a slap at the rest of us who were diligently eating five fruits and vegetables every day and working out and yet would never reach these proportions without tipping over and hurting ourselves.

This politically correct philosophy, however, hadn't stopped me from playing with Barbie as a little girl, when I had a wonderful time making up stories that starred her and her husband, as portrayed by my green plastic ruler from school. The ruler and Barbie did many wicked things together, including robbing banks, engineering bogus land deals, having sex with other school supplies—and once they gave birth to a pink eraser, whom they neglected while they vacationed behind the living room couch, otherwise known as Europe.

Nowadays I am way too tired to fight Barbie. Because of that malaise that comes from giving birth to three children and then allowing them to remain living with us, we were too exhausted to enforce a lockout on all the various Barbie Items. This explains why we are now knee-deep in Barbie paraphernalia—kicking her sports car out of the way so we can climb into the shower, moving her dream house off the couch when we want to watch television, and sharing the dining room table with her outfits, her dishes, and, of course, her zillions of pairs of shoes, of which there is not one single matching pair. In our house, there are Barbie shoes lurking everywhere you look. Billions and billions live in the couch cushions, under the refrigerator, and in the corners of the children's rooms, of course. You'd expect that. But how to explain the Barbie shoes in the humidifier? Or in the flour canister? Nestled next to your toothbrush? The only explanation is that these shoes are obviously having sex when we're not looking and are gleefully reproducing at a very rapid rate. They would be what scientists call a "successful species."

Barbie herself has even proliferated. When I was a child, we were content to own either the bubble-haired Barbie or the one with the swinging ponytail (no one had *both;* why would anyone ever require *two* Barbies? And where would the husbands come from?), nowadays there is a Barbie for every philosophy of life, profession, and geographical location. Every household has more of them than can be counted—and many, I'm sad to say, are headless. Yes, naked Barbie torsos populate the landscape in the average American ranch house, and I've not been surprised to run into the occasional Barbie arm or leg tossed in among the pots and pans. Probably it's there searching for shoes.

I do not know what the answer is to the Barbie Question: Whether to Give In or Not. You will have to look elsewhere, in books where wiser people than I can give you a definitive answer on how to keep Malibu Barbie and Gas Station Barbie out of your home and away from your children's delicate psyches. Perhaps you'll want to adopt the method my friend Elaine uses, where Barbie is concerned. She has repealed the Barbie boycott she enforced for many years—too many people were mad that she wouldn't let her kids accept their birthday presents—but she does insist on giving her kids a tiny little speech upon each new Barbie arrival. It's a boring speech, really. I've heard it a million times. It has to do with how those minuscule Barbie feet could never physically support those sticklike legs and those gigantic breasts, and then it goes into the Self-Esteem Diatribe, how we all have to accept ourselves the way we are, even though no one can ever look like Barbie, and, in fact, how we shouldn't try to.

Elaine calls it the Anorexia Prevention Barbie Speech, and afterward, just to make sure her kids really paid attention, they all sit down to doughnuts and hot chocolate, just to show they're not striving for one-inch waists or anything like that.

I have to admit that Barbie is a lot more palatable when you're eating a glazed doughnut.

Breast-feeding the trucks at day care

Okay, you've known for a long time that no matter how much you try to raise boys and girls alike, there's some very definite differences. A boy, for instance, would never think of refueling the day-care trucks by breast-feeding them—whereas a girl thinks that's really the most efficient, natural way, being what Mother Nature intended and all. And a girl pushing a car along the floor of her day-care center is no doubt driving it to the grocery store and the dry cleaners, while a boy needs to fling it around the room, alternating between making vrooming noises and sirens, so he can portray the excitement of the Indy 500 on a day all the cars blow up at once.

I once belonged to a cooperative day-care center, and we collectively believed we could single-handedly change the next generation of male-female dynamics simply by crossing out sexist references in books, forbidding certain sitcoms to ever be watched on television, and keeping Barbie and all toy guns far, far away. But let me just tell you this: You can make the Three Little Pigs into dynamic female characters, rename Bert and Ernie Roberta and Ernestina, and hang posters of Rosie the Riveter everywhere—yet still there's going to come the day when your darling little boy picks up a baby doll leg and makes a gun out of it and tries to shoot out the lights in the living room. And your daughter, seeing that blasphemy taking place, will let out a shriek loud enough to shatter glass in every home in the three closest counties.

My friends and I, the day-care moms, were diligent in making sure our children had only the most neutral and nonsexist puzzles and games to play with. I think we were the only people in America supporting a counterculture puzzle company that showed women in all high positions—lawyers, judges, doctors, mechanics, firefighters—and men always as the customers or the housekeepers. We were so proud of ourselves for locating these divine examples of just how the world *could* be—until one day one of the four-year-old boys cleared his throat and asked politely, "Ummm, can boys grow up to be lawyers, too?"

Even so, none of this gender-changing among the toys and books made any real lasting changes to male-female relations in the world—and probably none in these children's psyches either. The girls still put paper napkins on their heads at the snack table and declared they were brides, and one girl, wearing a pink tulle prom dress that someone had donated to the Dress-up Corner, once cooed at me, "Wouldn't it be nice if women didn't know how to drive, and men had to take them everywhere?"

Sometimes I think kids say these things just *because* they love to see the way your eyes bug out of your head and your eyebrows start leaping around on your forehead and you start to sprout warts. They take a moment to observe the curious changes happening in your face, and then placidly trot off to resume their life of spilling oatmeal on the baby doll beds.

Fine, you think. *But when you grow up, just see if you're not thrilled to be able to drive your own car. And trust me, you won't want to breast-feed it when it runs out of gas, either.*

While you wait for them to play Scrabble with you, how about . . . Candy Land?

For reasons none of us know, the toy companies have a vendetta against parents. This is the only way to explain that they invent games for little children that involve little colored pieces of plastic moving across a piece of cardboard, in a race to the finish line. I'm not sure if it's because their toy engineers are all old people who are jealous of how young people get to have a lot of sex and reproduce themselves, or if perhaps the companies have been paid off by space aliens who fear the energy and intelligence that people could harness if only their brain cells weren't being forced to play Candy Land all the time. But there you have it: billions and billions of these games are sold every year. I think every family in the United States has at least three of them, or at least a couple of the markers.

The first problem with Candy Land, as you will see, is that there has to be a winner and a loser. In other words, you can be sure that within thirty minutes of opening the box, someone is going to be screaming in tears and knocking over the board and all its pieces. And this person just might be you, which will make you feel like an idiot. It's tough to lose Candy Land five times in a row and keep your poise, believe me. Chances are, though, it's going to be your child who loses, at least some of the time, and he will make you feel like the Wicked Witch of the West who has robbed him of his chance at a happy childhood. Oh, you will be sorry, so sorry, to win at Candy Land.

It's your job, of course, to teach him to lose gracefully, that it's—ha-ha—"only a game" and that it's *fun* to play, whether you win or lose. This is one of those Lifelong Lessons that you know you are supposed to be working on, little by little, for the next twenty or so years, or until the kid gets his own apartment and some sympathetic friends. And even after he's grown, I think you're legally supposed to bring it up occasionally, like a recertification test to make sure he really got it.

But here's the thing: When he's four years old and coming face to face with the fact that his own mother will whip his butt at Candy Land, there's not much you can do to get the it's-fun-even-if-you-lose lesson truly implanted. You'll be lucky if he's not rampaging through the house, heaving figurines off the shelves and smashing the cereal bowls into bits and pieces. You can't very well run behind him at a time like that, shouting, "Now, now, we have to learn to be a good loser!"

No, at some point in your Candy Land Career, you will find yourself throwing games. You'll misread the dice, claim it's not really your turn and that your child must roll again, or even, in tough cases, make up new rules as you go along—all just to make sure your child wins so that the world can continue to spin correctly on its axis.

There are other rough parts to Candy Land besides the win-lose aspect, and the fact that it will turn you into a person who's no better than the 1919 Chicago White Sox, when they intentionally lost the World Series. I personally think the game inventors should be sent to their rooms for putting those pictures of candy canes and gumdrops all over the board. These put anyone in the mood for sticky, red-striped foods instead of the things you have competently stored in your cupboard for nourishing your family. No one has ever finished a game of Candy Land, and said, "How about we go finish up that leftover squash from the other night?" You will be lucky if you can even remember *anything* from the four food groups within twelve hours of finishing a Candy Land game.

The main Candy Land dilemma, though, is that the

games are endless. And when I say endless, I'm talking in terms of global events such as the Ice Age and the Ming dynasty. No, Candy Land is technically longer than the Ming dynasty. And the entire time that dinosaurs roamed the earth? Nothing compared to a single game of Candy Land on a rainy afternoon.

Yet children, as you will see, have plenty of time for a lifetime of Candy Land. They cheerfully finish one game, especially one that they've won—not noticing that you have grown stooped over and now have long gray hair—and suggest that now *you* be the green piece. "Let's see if you can win if you use the green," they will say, smiling at you expectantly.

"Aren't you at least thirty-five years old by now?" you are tempted to ask. "Shouldn't you be off at work and raising your own children?"

They will smile at you quizzically, certain that you're just trying to get out of playing one more game. It is this attempt to hide from Candy Land, more than anything else, that leads parents to insist on naptime for their kids—year after year after year, all the way until they're teenagers and won't get out of bed anyway.

Toy fads you never planned to fall for

There's something else about toys you need to know. It's a law of life in our society that every couple of years or so the industrialized nations all secretly get together and vote on a toy fad to drive parents insane. You would think nations would be too busy running their governments and figuring out taxation strategies to mess much with odd little toy collections, but that's the way it is. For weeks on end, nothing noteworthy takes place on any of the national news shows except lines of people desperate to get to a cash register so they can purchase the Thing All Children Must Have.

You think, before you have children, that you will be eminently able to resist these fads. It will be a point of pride with you and your child that you don't fall for these media binges.

This is a very healthy way to feel, before you have a child who is old enough to beg. And beg. And beg. And beg.

I am not proud of this, but I'm a veteran of many such toy rampages, and I can tell you that each one is more unbelievable than the one before it.

Things were bad, of course, when we as a people were forced to stand in line at toy stores to buy Cabbage Patch dolls. These were ugly little stuffed pieces of flannel stitched together on a plastic head that had scrunched-up features. Standing in line trying to purchase one of the limited number of these dolls, one might realize that it would be relatively easy to make one of these at home: grab some pajama material and then half melt a normal baby doll's plastic head in the oven and then put the two together.

But no. The sheer hideous facial expressions weren't enough, by themselves, to ensure this doll a place on every family's Must-Have list. The toy company had thoughtfully included a slip of paper telling you the doll's name, *in advance*, and claiming that this doll had actually been born in their factory, and that you, the consumer, were simply adopting their own beloved baby. God knows who the moms were supposed to be. The slip of paper didn't mention that part.

Our Cabbage Patch baby was named Bethany Heather. Her nickname, after the first week, was Beth Heth—and after that, no one ever called for her at all, because she had apparently decided to live facedown at the bottom of the toy box.

Still, odd as the Cabbage Patch craze was, it was nothing compared to the idiocy of standing in line to purchase pogs.

These were little cardboard disks with pictures on them, and people with small children were required to go out into stores and purchase them by the boxload.

Our family, I'll admit, was slow to jump on the pog bandwagon. We just couldn't figure out for the longest time what they were *for*. Finally a friend of mine, whose daughter was the Queen of Pogs for the Eastern States, I think, told me that pogs represented the past. They were, she said, designed to resemble the caps that went inside bottles of milk, back when milk was still delivered in bottles by the milkman.

"But we never saved *those* little caps," I said. "Why do we have to save things that now remind us of those little caps?"

She didn't know. Her family had never even had a milkman, and all her life she thought milk came from cardboard cartons anyway.

"Not cows?" I said. "Were you so far into the city that they didn't bother to explain to you about cows?"

"What are you, the toy police?" she said. "You just go out and buy your kid some of these cardboard disks, all right? They're cheap and they come in a canister where they can be contained, and they're not so hard to clean up even when they're spread all over the room."

"But I just don't see why anyone would want them!" I said. "They're useless and dumb, and they don't mean anything."

"Look," she said. "Your parents will be impressed that your children feel nostalgic for the days of milk bottle caps. They will buy all the pogs your child ever needs, and that will create a bond between your kids and your parents. And your kids will spend hours sorting and trading these disks, learning their colors and the useful properties of cardboard. You will have some peace and quiet for a little while each day while they are doing this. Now do you get it?"

I do. I get it. We bought tons of pogs. The craze lasted approximately fifteen more minutes, and then the dog ate the pogs and the canisters.

But just for the record, my parents didn't remember ever saving milk bottle caps.

Stuffed animals everywhere you look

Your relatives and friends believe that children need to have plenty of stuffed animals to keep them company in life. You can protest all you want that *you* are keeping your child company—but the stream of fuzzy bears, puppies, ducks, and stray elephants coming into your house will be never-ending just the same, starting at the baby shower and continuing until you threaten to call the legal authorities.

Stuffed animals, like some other household objects, are fond of reproduction, and are quite successful at it. Right now at my house, despite the fact that we originally opened our home to only about two thousand stuffed animals, we now have about 100 million of them. They are shoved into a hammock that is slung from the ceiling in one of the kids' rooms. We had to buy this hammock device because we had run out of floor space to hold all the stuffed animals, and several family members had sprained ankles from trying to wade through them or leap over them to get back and forth from the kitchen to the bathroom.

Frankly, life had become rather intolerable. We were using stuffed animals as couch cushions, as bed pillows, as superabsorbent paper towels—and once I even found a telephone message scrawled with Magic Marker into the belly fur of a blue bunny. But it wasn't until the foundation of the house started to crack that we realized our lives were endangered by these stuffed animals, and so we hauled about three truckloads to the Salvation Army. We suggested to the man who accepted them that he make sure this particular batch was separated as soon as possible since they were so highly sexed. I was sure they were part of a plot to take over the world.

But the four stuffed animals left behind wasted no time in creating even more replacements—and of course the friends and relatives, not responding to the court's restraining orders, kept sending more, and so now we have surpassed our household's safety level once again. Just yesterday I noticed a crack in the ceiling that may have been caused by the bulging, overwhelmed hammock.

I do not know what the answer is. I think eventually someone shall have to start a clothing fad that will consist of the pelts of stuffed animals all sewn together. We shall all be seen out in the cold with our plush pastel patchwork sweaters—some with bunny ears and elephant trunks poking out of them, and some with those plastic snouts and button eyeballs.

Stranger things have happened in the clothing industry, you know.

The very worst toys

Someone asked me recently which toy was the worst one I ever lived through. At first I thought it might have been the toy electric guitar, the sound of which made my nerves fray, unravel, and then splatter out onto the carpet. When my four-year-old played it (which she did all the time), she adopted a new persona, Miss Commanda. This name meant somehow that we could be commanded to listen to her play the guitar during every available second of the day, while she made up songs that went like this:

"Oh, I'm just a girl in a room.
And I like my toenail polish because it's red.
And sometimes I like black toenail polish,
But Mommy says no, black looks sick.
Maybe someday pink.
And then I scream.
AAAUUUUUGGGGGHHHH!!!!
The dog wanted to go to Burger King
But dogs can't go there unless they don't get sick in
    the car,
So he stayed home
And ate the curtains instead.
Barney says don't let the water run
When you brush your teeth
But I say, who cares about that?
My mommy says a pot is boiling on the stove,
But I say, who cares about that either?
Hey! Where are you going?
I need you to keep clapping!"

You can see that any toy that requires you to stay in one place, damage your ear drums, *and* clap is a very unfortunate toy indeed and shouldn't be purchased from the store without a note from your doctor saying you have a neurological system that can withstand this kind of abuse.

But even though the electric guitar was hideously loud, it was *not* the worst toy we ever bought. Nor was the Easy-Bake oven that never once managed to produce even one measly done-all-the-way-through cupcake. Or even the Silly Putty that got in everybody's hair and forced us all to get butch cuts.

No, the worst toy by far was Baby Heather, a Christmas present to our four-year-old. This wasn't Beth Heth, our Cabbage Patch doll, whose only real crime was her scrunched-in face and her exorbitant price tag. Baby

Heather was a large, pink plastic two-year-old doll that came equipped with many life-imitating skills. She didn't *need* the security of a birth certificate and adoption papers from the toy company. She had genuine batteries—four AA batteries and four C batteries, to be exact—and she was determined to run the household.

Christmas was barely over when I found myself in an argument with her. She was demanding that I put on her shoes.

"Put shoes on," she said twenty times in a row.

At first I didn't answer her, because frankly I was still in the phase of life where I prided myself on being able to tell the difference between actual children and plastic models of children. But after the thirteenth "Put shoes on" I heard myself say, "No, Heather, I'm busy right now." Then I said, "Anyway, I don't see why you think you need your shoes on when you're not going anywhere."

At the nineteenth "Put shoes on" I growled, "Will you leave me *alone!* Don't you know you're a *doll?*"

Finally I went over and pushed that magic spot on her belly that caused her to go off to a state the toy company called "sleep" in the brochure.

But guess what. In the interest of realism, those rascally toy designers had decided Baby Heather should go kicking and screaming into her enforced nap time. As soon as I pressed the button, she started whimpering and whining, and then broke into sobs.

"Baby not sleepy!" she hollered. "No sleep! No sleep!"

Then, just as a real toddler would, she tried one last trick: "Read story, Mama," before she finally, thankfully, closed her mechanical little eyes and shut up for good.

I went to read the brochure and learned that she had a vocabulary of 350 words—most of them bad-mannered complaints.

When my four-year-old daughter came and woke her up

later, I could hear Baby Heather wheedling in the other room: "Plaa-aaay with me, Mama." First she wanted a game of horsey, then pat-a-cake, then to color a picture. Then she wanted her hair combed, which she asked for in the most obnoxious way: "Mama, comb my hair. Mama, I'm pretty. Mama, get my shoes on. Mama, comb my hair again. Mama, I'm pretty."

All day long, my daughter fetched shoes, colored pictures, and played pat-a-cake. I knew just what she was feeling when she brought the doll in and said to her, "Here, play with your grandmother for a while!"

To make my daughter happy, I rocked this whiny piece of pink plastic for a few minutes while it bellowed instructions and flapped its eyelids at me.

But as soon as my daughter went outside to play with a stuffed animal who didn't talk back, I found myself thinking, *What the hell am I doing?* and put the doll in the back bedroom and closed the door.

And I cheered when the batteries went dead. Especially when my daughter didn't ask for replacements.

Don't name the Mylar balloons

Every now and then, through no fault of your own, Mylar balloons will come to live at your house. People seem to take great amusement in giving them to children. Take it from me: it's best if you can manage to throw them out the same day they arrive. They are not like ordinary balloons that hang around for a day or so, and then start to droop until they're mostly scudding along under the beds and getting smaller every day. A Mylar balloon—shiny and made of material so durable it should be used to manufacture space shuttles—will last for approximately the rest of your life. And, worse, it will chase you around the house.

I know, I know. Mylar balloons are simply inanimate objects—but you won't feel that way once they are chasing you. That's when, despite their smiling faces and friendly printed messages, you see they have quite discernible, even hostile, personalities. They rush at the front door when you come home, for instance, and always seem to be just outside the bathroom door when you emerge. They float along in the hall, grinning at you while you're brushing your teeth and getting ready for bed—and then if you rush downstairs to make sure you locked the front door, they think nothing of leaping ahead of you and then scaring you to death as you round the corner.

People will tell you that Mylar balloons don't have any evil intentions, that it's only because they're filled with air that they're very prone to float along on the prevailing breeze in the house. But once the balloons have tried to crowd you out from seeing your very own television set by hovering there just in front of the screen, you will begin to see that it can't be just coincidence that they are everywhere you want to be.

And frankly, at first it doesn't bother you that Mylar balloons are dogging your every move. In fact, you see them as there to greet you, and you are—well, why not admit it—you're flattered that a mere *thing* is so glad to see you that it would stop its aimless drifting to come greet you. You say something like, "Hi, there, Mr. Shiny Guy and Mr. Congratulations," not knowing you have just sealed your own fate. It's the cardinal rule of Thing Ownership that once you have bestowed a name on an object, it is yours and will stay with you forever. You will never be able to simply toss these characters into the garbage can. Otherwise, your child will be out there, wailing in the dark: "No, Mommy, not Mr. Shiny Guy! Not Mr. 'gratulations! They're our friends, Mommy!" (Balloons always try to get to the children first.)

I remember explaining to my husband that Mr. Shiny

Guy, particularly, was beginning to freak me out. One morning I stepped into the shower, only to find him already there, lurking behind the curtain. I could swear he was leering at me, with his beady little eyes in that big, pink smiley face.

"I wouldn't mind if Mr. Congratulations came into the shower, because he just has that pleasant red banner and doesn't have that all-knowing expression on his face," I explained to my husband. "He seems nice."

"Well, last night when I was trying to watch the NCAA finals, it was Mr. Congratulations I had the most trouble with," my husband said. "He kept getting in front of the TV screen, until finally I had to put him in the kitchen."

"How did you get him to go?"

"I had to actually walk him into the kitchen. Then I slowly slipped back to the TV, so he wouldn't notice."

"He didn't follow you?"

"No. He seemed to understand I'd had it with him."

"Hmmm. That may be why some of the ice cream was missing," I said. "Do you think he could get into the freezer without help?"

"I think these balloon boys could do anything," he said. "I saw Mr. Shiny Guy hovering around the banking stuff the other day, and I had to shoo him away before he started cashing our checks."

"I think it's time for us to lose these balloons. I can't live like this. I'm going to have a heart attack if one of them jumps out at me again."

"But the kids—what will we tell them?"

"Well, I don't think we can risk telling the truth on this one. You don't want the kids to get paranoid."

In the end, it took moving to completely rid us of our Mylar balloon ordeal. We tried throwing them out in the garbage a few times, but they always made it back into the house. Once the garbage man himself brought them to the back door, saying, "Surely you didn't mean to throw *these* away!" Another time the kids found them stashed underneath a bag of rotten oranges and saved them from being hauled away on the garbage truck.

And there were other times that I swear the balloon boys managed to seep their way back into the house even after they had been driven two blocks away on the truck. It's just a theory I have. But what finally worked was moving and leaving them in the old house. When I last saw them, they were still bobbing around next to the bathtub, waiting for the new tenants so they could scare the wits out of them.

11

Just Some of the 437 Questions

- Where is that man going?
- Why is that lady fat?
- Why do people ride in blue cars?
- Well, why is *that* man riding in a blue car?
- Do daddies have hair when they're babies?
- Do seahorses have noses?
- Do bad guys know they're bad guys?
- Did their mothers tell them they're bad guys?
- When a cow says "moo," did he think he really said "hi"?
- What if a giant ate up all our dinner and we didn't get any?
- When will I be older than you?
- Why is there pizza?
- Why can't a girl have a penis, too?
- Why do bees want to bite children?
- What is eight plus five plus eighteen plus twenty-two plus three?
- Why do bees want children to eat honey?
- If bees like honey, would they like syrup, too?
- Do bees' mommies ever make them pancakes?

- How does Santa Claus know where new babies live?
- Why is my left knee saltier than my right one?
- What time is zero-thirty?
- What if we could eat rocks for supper?
- Would rocks taste good then?
- Can a butterfly be a bird sometimes?
- Can you put houses on pizza?
- Are we real or is somebody dreaming of us?
- Can cars ride on pizza roads?
- If cats wore clothes, would our cat wear a dress or pants?
- Do cats wish they could bark like dogs?
- Do dogs want to drive cars by themselves?
- Can I ever fly?
- Why do we have to sleep?
- What if my name was Camilla Terrible?
- Would that mean I would act terrible?
- If I went in the forest, would I have to eat porridge?
- Would you still know me if I didn't have the same name I have?
- Where is that boy going?
- I think that boy looks like his name is Dragon. What do you think his name is?
- Does God have a belly button?
- I wrote these letters. What do they say? R-T-N-Z.
- Well, don't letters make words?
- What is Tuesday?
- Can I ride in the washing machine when it spins around?
- How many Band-Aids is too many for one cut?
- What does the newspaper say?
- Why was I crying when I was born?
- Do they put children in jail if they make a mistake and bite somebody?

- Do dogs go to jail if they bite somebody?
- What will you do when Daddy and I get married?
- Where was I before I lived with you?
- When I was a baby living in your tummy, did you think about naming me Larissa?
- Didn't you think I would be a nice baby if I was named Larissa?
- Why do people crash cars?
- Why do police carry sticks?
- Did you know my name when I was born?
- Do sharks ever come out of the water?
- Why is Barney purple?
- What is bread for?
- Why is my pillow soft?
- Do dogs know my name?
- Do cars drink gas or eat it?
- Why can't I wear Daddy's shoes to school?
- What time is forever?
- If I was an ant, how long would it take me to walk around my bed?
- What's the opposite of ice cream?
- Why does the computer turn on slow?
- Do chocolate chip cookies know they look like pieces of poop?
- Do squirrels like horses?
- How many birds are there in the world?
- Do fishes go swimming with lobsters?
- How many toes do all the monkeys in the world have?
- Are the stars the same hot in the nighttime as the daytime?
- Why do daddies drink coffee?
- Do bugs say hello to each other?
- Does Santa Claus make Barbie dolls?
- If I ask Santa Claus to bring Mrs. Claus with him, do you think he would say okay?

- Why don't swings ever go over the top?
- When you're the baby and I'm the mommy of you, will you still fix the dinner?
- Would you be mad if somebody wrote on the couch with Magic Marker?
- Would Santa Claus be mad if somebody wrote on the couch with Magic Marker?
- Does Santa Claus know the Tooth Fairy?
- What name does he call her—Tooth or Mrs. Fairy?
- Does the Tooth Fairy give the teeth to new babies?
- How does Santa Claus get in the house if you don't have a chimney?
- Do people give him a key to all the houses?
- What is that rabbit's last name?
- If animals don't have last names, then what about Bob Cat?
- If Santa Claus can't find the keys to the sleigh, do kids get any presents?
- How many times will you sneeze in your life?
- How many times will Daddy sneeze?
- Did your grandma tell you how many times she sneezed?
- What's the name of this dust?
- Well, why doesn't dust have a name?
- What does "sex" mean?
- Does Minnie Mouse play minigolf?
- Why does Daddy say "shit" when the light turns yellow?
- Were dolls ever real children?
- When I grow up and get babies, can they sleep with us in your bed?

12

Monsters, Bugs, and the Threat of Shampoo

Monsters under the bed, behind the toilet, and in the heating vents

Once you knew how many monsters are loose in the world, but for years now you probably haven't been keeping track of them. Not to worry. Luckily you have a little child now to point them all out. In our house, many of the objects that I thought were just ordinary household items were actually prone to morphing into scary things. The ceiling fan, for instance, was often changing into a monster—and more times than I can count, ghosts took over one of the dresser drawers, making it difficult for regular people to sleep in the same room with them. Naturally we didn't want to give in to this kind of thinking, but there were times when, at 2:00 A.M., it seemed easier to move the ghost-infested dresser out into the hallway than to argue about it.

We've had witches in the radiators, evil goblins gurgling in the bathtub drain—and for a while, at least, a strange sort of spirit who hovered around the dryer vent and managed to spew dust and hot air on people. I did my best to persuade my child that these weren't *real*, but nothing I said on the subject had much credibility since it had been discovered that I didn't think cartoon characters were *real* either, and how to explain Mickey Mouse himself walking around in Disney World? ("That's a person dressed up in a

Mickey Mouse costume," I said, but that explanation was considered feeble and even laughable. Anyone could see that was really Mickey, because otherwise, he'd have on a regular person's shoes—and he had *huge* shoes.)

My kids were somehow born with their fears already intact. I suspect that even in the delivery room, they were noticing all the possible safety issues: Am I too slippery? Is this doctor likely to drop me on my head on the hard floor? Did that nurse wash her hands? They probably suspected there were monsters there, too, hiding behind the big light above us, or else lurking in the nursery. Surely that was why everybody in there was shrieking.

Many things were found to be hideously scary during those first few days: bathing, getting undressed, getting dressed again, diaper changes, air currents. Then there were their inborn mammalian fears of starving to death, being dropped on the floor, and running out of mucus. (It's my theory that babies believe that mucus is their only easily obtainable commodity, and they are very worried about its disappearance. This explains a lot of that nonspecific crying during the first few months: they're anxious about running out, so they cry to make sure they can still produce the stuff.)

My kids gradually accepted the idea that they were going to be able to manufacture plenty of wet, sticky stuff to use whenever they wanted to glue substances together, and moved on to other fears. We moved steadily through witches, ghosts, monsters, bad guys, and train wrecks—and then when he was five, my son woke me up in the middle of the night to ask if we had insurance.

"Of course we do," I said in my sleep. "We've got lots of insurance."

"How much?" He had his worried face on.

"Enough. We carry what the insurance company recommends. Now go back to bed."

"But what if something really really big happens? What if the whole house gets sucked up by a tornado and lands on somebody else's house? Would our insurance pay for two houses?"

"I think so."

Long silence. Then: "I think we should call them and ask."

"We are not calling our insurance company in the middle of the night."

"Do you *hear* that wind blowing outside?" he said. "Do you know for sure that the house is going to stay on the ground?"

"What I do know for sure is that I'm going to be way too crabby tomorrow if I don't get any more sleep tonight," I said. "*That* should be your main worry tonight—that you're going to be stuck tomorrow with a mother who's in a bad mood all day."

After he left and went back to bed—ten rough minutes later—I said to my husband, "How do you suppose he knows about insurance? Could *Sesame Street* be teaching this stuff?"

"When you're a born worrier, you make it your business to know about things like insurance," my husband said. "He probably overheard some nurses talking about it when he was a newborn, and he's been mulling it over all this time. He's got a lot of things he's pondering for the future. The other day he asked me if I'd help him when he has to write an essay for college, and if I thought he'd get arthritis from cracking his knuckles."

We laughed, but after everybody finally got back to sleep, I lay there awake—yes, worrying about the wind blowing outside and whether our insurance really is adequate—and by 4:00 A.M., I'd moved on to those troublesome college essays, knuckle cracking, and, worse, wondering how I'd managed to raise such a worrier.

The age of irrationality

I have to warn you now: Nothing about your child's fears will make much sense to you. You probably can relate to the scariness of being left behind in a crowded shopping mall or falling from the top of a high slide in the playground or, let's see, going so high on the swings that you flip over the top of the bar and land on your head on the ground. I'm afraid that none of these fears has ever occurred to your child.

No, when he's wailing away in abject terror, he's decided that the feathers in the down comforter are after him.

My friend Katherine's kid was terrified of button-down shirts. He would cry and scream whenever she tried to put one on him, or when she tried to wear one herself. "No buttons! No buttons!" It was heartrending to watch, and to hear him scream you'd think she was exposing him to something truly dangerous like bubbles in the bubble bath—which my own daughter was afraid of—or that somebody had stirred up some dust motes, which were whirling about in a frightening sort of way.

But no, it was just the buttons.

"What do you think it is about the buttons that scares him?" I asked her one day. In those days, I had little to do but fixate on such things as other people's children's irrational fears. I think it made me feel better about my own children, who were at that moment hiding behind the couch, worrying about the humming of the fluorescent light in the kitchen. "Is it the plastic disks themselves, or the fact that he can't button them up without help?"

She gave me a steady, tired gaze. "Does it matter?"

Later, the moms who hung out in the park and who had time for psychoanalyzing each other's children figured out that it had to do with his weaning. Katherine had breast-fed him until he was two years old, at which point he had been willing to go on forever, it seemed, while she had gotten concerned that maybe he'd *never* stop on his own. She wasn't just being paranoid either. One day he had asked her how breast-feeding would work out after he was married. Did she think his wife would want nursing, too? And just how would they go about that—one side for each of them, or should they perhaps take turns? Or maybe his wife's mother would want to be involved.

Katherine got so freaked out at just the mere suggestion that she would ever nurse two *adults*, one of them not even related to her, that she just abruptly closed down the Breast-Feeding Establishment and took to wearing tucked-in, button-down shirts with high collars instead of the nice, loose shirts she was forever pulling up for him.

Obviously she had ruined her little boy for any career in which a good shirt is a prerequisite, and the moms in the park clucked over this for a long time. Meanwhile, our own little kids, romping in the sandbox, ate dirt, leaped off the high slide, swung upside down on the trapeze—and yet cowered in fear when little Johnny's down jacket sprang a leak and some feathers got stuck to his sweatshirt.

The Moms' Psychoanalytic Society in the Park worked on that one for quite a while: had our children been frightened by ducks? Had Saturday morning television cartoons ever featured evil poultry figures harming young kids? Were the Perdue people to blame somehow?

After a lengthy discussion, we finally came up with a professional opinion: kids' fears make no sense at all.

Explaining about bad guys without scaring everybody to death

I'm sorry, but the law requires today that all parents tell little kids about bad guys. The technical term is "stranger danger," and by the time children are three or so, you're supposed to let them know that they shouldn't go off with just anyone.

I will tell you right now that I was not very good at getting this concept across, although I can't for the life of me understand how I got it so wrong. While other people were merrily hauling their kids down to the police station to be fingerprinted and photographed in case they ever got kidnapped, I was barely able to cover the rudiments of taking-candy-from-strangers without inducing uncontrolled hysteria.

And I brought up the subject so delicately, too.

I said, "You know, when we're out in public, it's kind of important that you stay close beside me."

The kid said, eyes suddenly wide: "Why?"

"Welllll . . . so you won't get lost."

"Lost? Why would I get lost? And what would happen to me if I got lost?"

"Well, it's just that I wouldn't know where you were, and—"

"You wouldn't *see* me?"

"No, and somebody else might want you to go with them—"

"You mean bad guys?"

"Well. I guess you could say they were bad guys. Yes."

"AAAUUUGGHH! Oh, no! Bad guys would come and take me away, and I'd never see my home again! And they'd probably hurt me and make me do all the work! They'd have scary faces and they wouldn't be nice to me and make me birthday cakes!"

This, I know, is not the mood you're striving for when you have a talk about the realities of modern life. Here I had not even gotten to the parts that the police definitely want you to cover—how sometimes strangers might try to lure a child away, so it's important that she knows how to scream loud, and who to run to for help. You also, the police say, should make sure your child knows her address and telephone number (area code is good if you're anticipating those out-of-state kidnappings).

I could see that I was not the person who could successfully suggest my child learn an appropriate scream. Besides, she was *already* screaming.

"Oh, no! There are bad guys in the world! I knew it! I knew it! I can't go anywhere anymore because the bad guys will get me! Oh, no, no, no!"

Like most parents, I had hoped I could merely give a nod to the subject that the world is not always the place we'd like it to be, and have all my rules agreed upon without any hysteria. Some friends of mine have had the opposite problem. They've been unable to impress upon their kids the reasons for safety concerns at all. My friend Marian actually had to mention the grossest possibilities: child slavery, kidnapping, and dismemberment, even bringing in scenes from horror movies she'd seen—only to have her kid chuckle, and say, "Oh, that not happen to me."

Not, however, in my family. Once a baby-sitter happened to mention to my child that sometimes strangers try to lure little children away with candy and ice cream, and for months after that, we talked about bad guys morning, noon, and night.

"What flavor ice cream do bad guys give kids?" I'd be asked. And when I'd try to shrug this off, I'd be hit with a barrage of questions. "Do bad guys know where little children live? Do they know where I live? Do they know what kind of ice cream I like? Do the ice cream stores always sell ice cream to bad guys? When the mans at the ice cream store sell ice cream to somebody, do they think this is a bad guy who is going to give it to a little child and take that child away? What if the ice cream melts before the bad guy gets to the child? Is that why they use candy sometimes?"

Naturally the most pressing of these questions arose at night around bedtime, when we were already battling the ghost-in-the-closet problem, the spiders-under-the-bed problem, and the lamp-on-the-dresser-turning-into-a-monster-when-the-light-went-out problem. With bad guys added in, bedtime became the kind of ordeal I had to rest up for beforehand.

One night my friend Liza asked if her three-year-old could spend the night at our house while she went into the city with her husband. That night, tucking the two little girls in, we did the two required bedtime stories, the four songs, the prayers, then the preemptive search for spiders, the reassurances about the dresser lamp and the closet ghost, and the daily discussions of bad guys' ice cream purchasing habits.

Then our guest, little Yvonne, piped up. "I need to know whether you have any werewolves in the house."

"No," I said firmly. "No, we have never had werewolves, and besides that, there aren't any such things as werewolves."

"I know there are werewolves," said Yvonne. "I've seen them."

I cast a worried glance over to my own child, in case this was going to end up being some turning point for her in the fear category. I didn't think it was going to be technically possible to add one more fear to the Worry List and still make it to bed in time for eight hours of sleep each night.

But my child was serene. "You don't have to worry about werewolves," she said.

I smiled at her, kissed them both, and tiptoed out.

"What you need to worry about," said my child, "is if

bad guys know what kind of ice cream you like. Now, you like chocolate, right? That's bad, because any bad guy could guess about that."

"There are no bad guys and no werewolves," I said from the hallway. "Good night!"

"If a bad guy ever asks *me* what kind of ice cream I like, I'm going to say rum raisin, because I don't think anybody really likes that kind, and he probably won't have it, so I won't have to go with him," said my child.

"Werewolves," said Yvonne, "don't care what kind of ice cream you like. They just eat you right up!"

"That's why I like to be afraid of bad guys," said my kid. "At least you get ice cream."

"There are no bad guys and no werewolves," I said again.

But no one was listening. Later, they both came and slept in my bed.

Bugs and the hourly bug census

At 10:00 A.M., there were *lots* of spiders on our front porch, two mosquitoes in the bathroom, a centipede in the hallway, three flies in the kitchen, a bazillion gnats swarming in the backyard, about 100 trillion ants in the pantry, and a bee with only one wing on the back steps.

This news was reported by our three-year-old, who then had to leave to make sure nothing had changed.

By 10:37, there were only five spiders on the front porch. (The others, to the census taker's great consternation, were missing; had they gone inside the house and were hiding, perhaps in someone's bedsheets?) The two mosquitoes had added a third and fourth, the centipede was now nestled against the wall, the flies had moved over to the dog food, the bazillion gnats were still all accounted for, the 100 trillion ants looked as though they'd called in some new recruits, and the bee with one wing didn't look like he was ever going anywhere, but he was now twitching.

Do you want to know what the bug situation was by 11:05? No? Oh, but if you're the parent of a three-year-old child, you must. Sometimes you will be taken away from very important business—dragged out of showers, even—to estimate the population of a certain group of insects and to ruminate over its destructive capabilities. ("Dad! Dad! Is that a jillion or a thousand flies, and if they tried to carry me, would they drop me on the ground?") There will be times when you will be asked to explain not only *why* there are so many bugs gathered in one place, but what their likely next move will be.

You have become a bug apologist. Even if you personally *hate* every specimen in the entire insect kingdom, you now find yourself having to defend their right to an existence. This is tough if, like my friend Elsa, you frankly think the world would be a vastly improved place if the bugs were off it. But it's either defend them or try to get rid of all of them single-handedly.

Nope, instead of taking on the entire insect kingdom, you will most likely elect to go to the library and check out positive books that tell how industrious insects are and all the wonderfully heroic things they have done for mankind. You must explain that they are really quite beautiful, that they have a purpose in life beyond just making people miserable. You will no doubt even one day buy Uncle Milton's Ant Farm and raise your own crop of store-bought ants, when you have perfectly adequate ants tromping daily through your kitchen. You will become—yes!—a cheerleader for spiders and a lecturer leading psychological discussions on the Misfortunes of the Much-Maligned House Fly.

No one will believe you that insects are wonderful, of course. But this is what parenthood drives you to: a kind of pathetic boosterism just so you won't constantly have to be leaping out of your chair and killing everything that crawls.

The bathtub chronicles

I don't mean to complain about Mister Rogers, whom I've always appreciated for liking my children just the way they are, but it must be said that he has done quite a bit of damage, fear-wise, to the process of bathing. I know he meant well, of course, but once he sang that song about how kids *won't* go down the drain, there hasn't been a toddler in America who's rested easily.

I myself had never known anyone who ever worried for one second about the possibility of being sucked down the drain, but by the time my son and I had listened to Mister Rogers's song, frankly we were *both* quaking over the idea. There was something in the tone of his voice that just seemed a little too insistent. Was there once a child who did manage to go down the drain, and is Mister Rogers merely trying to keep the true story from getting out and prevent mass hysteria? Is Fred Rogers a pawn of the powerful drain industry who has bought him off and written a song to mollify the rest of us?

The truth is that even without the dreaded Bathtub Drain Song, there is plenty about baths to be scared of, and your child will no doubt fixate on each one of them. He's not scared of the same things about the bath that *you* are, however. He will happily stand up on one foot while in the slippery tub, dance around, and throw sudsy water all over the bathroom floor, all without giving one minute's thought to whether his life is in danger.

No, his fears will concern something totally harmless: say, the wad of hair he once saw in the drain, the bubbles that form on the cake of soap, even his own reflection in the bathtub spout. My friend Ellie's three-year-old was inconsolable over the tiny black blobs he discovered in the tile grout.

"What those are?" he asked her, barely able to bring himself to point at them.

"Tiles," she said. "Bathtub tiles."

"No. That stuff."

She looked. "Oh, that's the grout between the tiles. It holds the tiles together." I think she knew at this point that he was talking about mildew, but Ellie is nothing if not an optimist. She attended the School of Motherhood that believes that you can just keep answering your child's questions with the answers to the questions you *wished* he had asked instead, and that eventually he will get tired of asking the same question over and over again. Mind you, this only rarely works with any child over the age of nine months, but Ellie sticks to this theory just the same. We, her friends, admire her for it very much.

"Grout," he said. Then, "Why grout is black?"

"Grout," she said cheerfully, "is white. It holds the tiles together and keeps them from falling off the wall. It's very good stuff. Not scary at all."

"But the black dots are scary. They not grout. That bad stuff."

"It's a little bit of stuff called mildew," she said. "Lots of tubs in America have mildew." Then she went on to explain that the current economic situation in this country has required that most families have two incomes, which has left little time for people to chase down mildew the way they once could. And how, even with two incomes, most people couldn't afford the household help that would help with eradication of such things as mildew, wrinkles in clothing, and dust motes landing on tables.

"People used to stay home and cook dinners, too," she said. "Nobody ever heard of microwaves or dinners you could cook in twenty seconds. Things took time, and people had the time. Now, that's what's scary," she told him. "Not the mildew itself. It's just a symptom of a much larger problem."

Her son just blinked at her.

"Well," she said to me later, "if he's going to have fears, he might as well be scared of the things that truly matter."

What they worry about in the middle of the night

- Men with black eyebrows
- Spiders on the back porch who are probably now sleeping under their pillow
- The fuzz from the blanket
- The curtain rod falling
- The floor boards creaking
- Someone climbing in the window, packing them up in a shopping bag, and taking them away
- The possible future death of Barney
- The gurgle of the bathtub drain from five hours ago

Things you can only wish they'd be scared of

Naturally you have your own fears. And let's face it, you wish your child would share in them.

Fat chance.

Oh, sure, every now and then someone produces a kid who seems to have come equipped with a realistic sense of danger. This is the kind of child who gleans, for instance, that automobiles are powerful, heavy machines that could do a lot of damage to a human body, and so he elects not to run in front of them. You are thrilled about this, but don't make the mistake of thinking that this natural caution came from your wise counsel on the subject of Car Dangers.

No one knows where this kind of fear comes from. Probably it's just another of those accidental programming glitches during your child's gamete phase, and while it is useful and wonderful, the downside of it often is that he's *so* terrified of cars that he won't ride in one without sedation. You will have to cajole and bribe and plead with him to get him to go anywhere at all.

My friend Jane had a kid who needed to know car seat safety specifications so that he could feel comfortable about automotive travel. There he was, just barely over three years old, and they were always talking about the bolts that held the car seat to the chassis of the car to keep it from flying through the windshield in case of impact.

That's the word she used—"impact"—because naturally with a kid like that, you have to be careful to avoid language like "wreck," "crash," or "accident." You have to represent auto travel as the most safe method of getting around that was ever devised while at the same time making clear that car seats and seat belts and harnesses are absolutely required.

There are plenty of things they *could* be scared of, which would make your life much easier, but no doubt they'll never get to any of these.

- Standing on one foot at the top of the sliding board
- Wanting to go higher on the swings, so high that the whole set groans and tries to get out of the cement that's holding it to the ground
- Walking along walls
- Standing up on roller coaster rides
- Lying on their backs eating crackers
- Sliding down banisters

- Catching sticks on fire
- Dashing across the street to reach the ice cream truck
- Throwing rocks in the air
- Spinning around with dish towels on their heads until they're so dizzy they crash into the furniture
- Cooking soup for themselves while you're on the phone
- Telling strangers where they live, your salary, and where you left your car keys
- Tasting chemicals they find under the sink
- Turning on the electric drill
- Running with lollipops in their mouths
- Walking downstairs blindfolded
- Running with the scissors
- Tasting marbles
- Cutting their own hair
- Sledding downstairs on their blankets
- Standing up in the car while it's moving
- Touching every object in a public rest room
- Rubbing against parked cars

Bad dreams

Once middle-of-the-night feedings are over, you may think you deserve to get a few years of uninterrupted sleep just to pay off some of that massive sleep debt you've accumulated since giving birth.

But then along come bad dreams.

Some people say that little kids have nightmares because they get so overstimulated during the day that they can't process all the information they've taken in, and so disturbing scenes play out in their unconscious minds while they slumber. Other, more hostile, people believe that it's your fault—and if you make the mistake of getting in a conversation with them, they'll drag out the fact that you let your baby cry herself to sleep when she was five months old. Remember that night when you were hoping she'd learn something about giving in to exhaustion, and instead she cried for four hours? Some people will remind you of that if you let them.

But I say nightmares are just the latest thing in an organized plan to keep you from ever getting any sleep. Add bad dreams to the list that already includes hunger, teething, boredom, ear infections, illness, pacifier losing, and tongue biting, and you will see that not until your child moves away to her own apartment will you truly ever be rested again.

This is why many parents you see these days walk stooped over and might tend to snap at you if you inquire why they're always in bad moods.

The trouble with your child's nightmares, besides the fact that they wake *you* up, is that there's no way to know exactly how to make the crying go away. I've found that children aren't particularly articulate in the middle of the night, and so you're often left to guess at the horrible event that must have happened in their little heads. Was it the famous being-chased-by-a-monster dream? Or perhaps ghosts? Scary reptiles? A swarm of ants perhaps? Did the guy with the abrasive voice who sells furniture on TV show up in their sleep and try to sell them a couch they couldn't write on with markers?

You'd like a clue before you start your comfort routine, because if you say, "There really aren't any such things as monsters," your child may look at you in alarm and start wailing all over again, having dreamed instead about a squirrel who scampered near her in the park four months ago, but now being quite ready to switch over to a fear of monsters since you've brought them up.

My friend Lydia used to march into her child's room, armed with a flashlight and a list of things she was ready to claim were not real, only to find out one night that her child was really screaming about bus exhaust. Yes, those clouds of smoke that happen around buses had made their way into her kid's nightmares—and, as Lydia said later, what can you really say that's comforting about bus exhaust?

About the best you can come up with is, "Luckily there's not any bus exhaust right here in this room, so you are perfectly safe to go back to sleep." And I guess I don't have to tell you that that's pretty lame when you're confronting a bona fide nightmare. Saying this doesn't really work with monsters, ghosts, and slithering reptile dreams either, but Lydia says it's completely inadequate against fear of bus smoke.

"What is he—a budding environmentalist or something?" I said. "Next he'll be waking up screaming about global warming and endangered tree toads."

"Maybe if I sent a check to Save the Planet, he could rest more easily," she said.

Sometimes you just have to wait out a nightmare. My own kids liked to get up and have a deep, full, all-lights-on discussion of whatever it was they had dreamed about, and once that was under way, they didn't see any reason why we shouldn't just stay up for the rest of the night and discuss lots of subjects that had been on their minds. We spent many of the wee hours sipping orange juice together in the kitchen and chatting about *Sesame Street* characters' personalities, weather patterns in the continental United States, and why God bothered to make asparagus.

Every now and then I'd suggest we make our way back to our beds, and that's when they'd get all wobbly again and start whimpering about the bad dream that was waiting for them there on the pillow.

"There are no bad dreams on the pillow," I'd say. "Bad dreams are in your head, and your head is all better now."

On truly desperate nights, I'd do a Dream Switch with them. That's where you offer to take on the nightmare, and offer them your dream instead, which you always claim is something like sailing along on a lovely little pond on a bright, sunny day with just enough breeze and white, puffy clouds in the sky.

"So I'll take the horrible lizards-and-snakes dream, and you're in this nice boat," I'd say, tucking them back in.

One time I had crawled back into bed, my head full of lizards, and was proudly sinking into a restful, if cold-blooded, slumber, when I heard my child screech from his bedroom.

"What happened?" I said.

"The little boat sank, and now a snake got in it," he yelled back.

"Just throw it out of the boat and swim for shore," I said. "I'm sure there's a nice picnic lunch for you there."

Later he called out that the sandwiches had mustard and onions on them, and that it was starting to rain.

That's when I fell back on my old standby. "If you don't go to sleep and stay that way until morning, I'm going to be so crabby that you'll have material for an entire month of bad dreams!"

At last . . . there was silence.

13

Yes, Virginia, There Is a Kindergarten

Okay, there's a kindergarten—but it only lasts for thirteen minutes a day

Kindergarten starts precisely five minutes before you're ready to go crazy. Your child has now asked you approximately 159,505 questions over the past year—and you are more than ready to hand over the answering responsibilities to a hired professional and go back to bed.

You've talked about why birds fly, the origin of belly buttons, and whether cats like the way they look in mirrors—and now you need some sleep. One of the major problems with kindergarten, of course, is that they don't hold it at night, when you could really benefit from some shut-eye hours. Instead, most likely it's during the time when you're already committed to being at work.

And, unlike having a day-care situation or a baby-sitter, kindergarten does not last all that long. For some reason, often your child is back home from kindergarten before you've even made your way from the bus stop back to your own home. And forget about driving him to school. Once you drop him off and drive back home, it's time to go back to school and pick him up. If you, say, decide to stop for gas or to mail a letter at the post office, by the time you head back to the school, your child will be forlornly waiting in the office, all the other children having gone home.

This makes no sense, of course. Half-day kindergarten should legally have to be half of a day—but instead, in most states, I think close scrutiny would reveal that it barely amounts to about thirteen minutes.

But trust me on this: In that thirteen minutes, they will manage to answer many of your child's questions, including whether or not seahorses have noses and why there is pizza. And that, eventually, will bring you some relief.

Kindergarten readiness

There's just one teeny tiny detail about kindergarten you need to know before you can pack your child off to it. The authorities want to know if your child is Ready.

They would like to give her a little, ah, test—just to make sure.

And they would like you to interrupt your otherwise un-eventful little life and head down to the school building with your child while they ask her some questions, check out her skill levels, and generally create a little anxiety, in case there's a shortage of that in your life right then.

Naturally, you become immediately terrified that your child will be found Unready, and that you are to blame. Why haven't you been working on her math skills? Why couldn't you have purchased the flash cards and the Mozart tapes and all the rest of it? What kind of parent are you, anyway? It's probably too late to run out and purchase some phonics program or the Spanish tapes. God—why have you lived such a shoddy, haphazard life?

Despite your failings, you broach the subject with your child as nonchalantly as you can manage. "Oh, by the way, we're going to school together this morning," you say when the day comes.

"School? I thought school didn't start yet," she says.

"It doesn't. We're going for a visit to the school."

"I don't want to visit the school."

"Oh, it'll be fun. We'll go in and talk to people, fill out your forms, answer a few questions—"

"What questions? What forms? Who do we have to talk to?"

"Well, I don't really know just yet. But it'll be fun."

"I'm not going to the school."

"But they want you to."

"You said I had to go in September. Is it September?"

"Not yet, but—"

"Then I don't want to go."

"Sweetheart, we got a letter from the school. (You want to say from the Kindergarten Readiness Militia, which is how you're thinking of them, but you stop yourself just in time.) All the kindergarten children are going in for a meeting first, to meet the teacher (you have no idea if she'll be meeting with the teacher), and to talk a little bit (you don't know if she'll be talking), and to answer some questions about how much you know." You rush through this last part just so maybe she won't notice.

But of course she does notice. "How much I know?! How much I *know*? What if I don't know enough? What if the things I know aren't the right things? What if I know something but I can't remember when they ask me? What if I don't talk loud enough? What if they already have too many children for the kindergarten, and they're just looking for somebody they can tell to stay home and not come to school this year?"

Since these are exactly your own fears, there's not much you can say. So you call up your friends who've gone through this particular torture, and ask them what to expect, and they all say, "Oh, it'll be fine, don't worry," and you tell your child that everybody else went through the same thing and it's just to help the teacher know how much she needs to teach you and how much she doesn't need to teach you because you already know it.

Kindergarten Readiness Testing varies. With each of my three children, there has been a different protocol. My oldest was led into a room where he met his actual kindergarten teacher, who was the nicest person in the universe, and they loved each other immediately. He would have moved in with her after just that one visit.

As part of the test, she placed about twelve objects on the table in front of him—chalk, a book, a pencil, a piece of paper, stuff like that—and then asked him to close his eyes while she removed one. When he opened his eyes, she said, "Now, which object is missing?"

He looked at her blankly. And then he said, "You didn't *tell* me I was going to need to turn my brain on for this."

From the way she laughed, I could see they were going to get along fine—and that my worst problem that year was going to keep her from starting adoption proceedings to get him away from us.

My second child was sent to the gymnasium, where tables were set up with different testers at each table. The would-be kindergartners were to move around the room, answering questions and trying out their skills as they moved along. Parents were sent to the library to quake with others, and to drink coffee.

On the drive home, my daughter was very solemn. "They asked me how high I could count," she said, "and I told them I could count up to one hundred twelve."

"Can you really?" I said.

She demonstrated.

"Do you know what comes next after one hundred twelve?" I said.

"What?" She sounded surprised that anything possibly could.

"One hundred and thirteen. And then one hundred fourteen . . ."

Her face lit up. "And then one hundred fifteen?"

"That's right."

"We've got to go back!" she said. "Turn the car around. They need to know I've got some new numbers."

"It'll be okay," I said. "We'll tell them on the first day of school."

At eleven o'clock that night, she was up, rubbing her eyes and worrying. "I can't sleep because I'm worried about something. I think the kindergarten needs to know the truth about my counting. I think maybe they won't let me go there if they think it's only one hundred twelve."

"They'll let you go there," I said. "I heard them say all the children are going to go."

"Please call them in the morning and tell them I got to one hundred fifteen."

"Sweetheart, we can't keep calling them for number after number. You're learning new numbers all the time, and they don't have to know about each one of them. They're busy people. Anyway, they just wanted to make sure you even knew what numbers *are*. Some kids probably can't count at all."

"Or maybe some kids can count to one, and then they can't think about what comes next," she said.

"Well, probably—"

"Okay," she said, taking a deep breath. "Just call them and say I'm up to one hundred twenty—because I will be when I think about it—and then tell them I'm still learning, and if they get a chance, they could call me back in the middle of next week and see what I'm up to. They could call when they're not too busy."

And off she went to bed.

Searching for Mr. Lunch Box

There's just one huge anxiety-producing scene left to you before school actually starts. Chances are, your child is going to have to pick out a lunch box.

This is one of those things that should be easy but which is fraught with peril. There are so many wrong lunch boxes out there in the world. You have no idea.

Here's a little of what he's going through: What if he picks a babyish lunch box and gets to school the first day and finds himself ridiculed? What if he picks a lunch box that is too sophisticated for his station in life as a kindergartner, and some fourth grader has to put him in his place? What if he picks the same lunch box as all the twenty-four other kids in his class, and he can't ever tell which one is his when they're all lined up in the closet? Then he might open somebody else's lunch box and instead of peanut butter and jelly there's something disgusting like roast beef with lettuce and tomato, and he'd have to eat *that*. He turns pale, just thinking about it.

You may have to go with him to the store and stare at lunch boxes for a very long time. You might want to take a book and a portable chair with you, so you won't be tempted to rush the process along. Get comfortable. This is not simply selecting something to carry his sandwich back and forth in, remember. While he's standing there, staring at the rows of lunch boxes, he's doing some very important psychological analysis on himself, perhaps for the first time in his short little life.

Is he the type for the *Star Trek* look, or is that pretentious for a five-year-old? Can he pull off an *X-Files* thing, or should he hold off until first grade to make that kind of statement? He *likes* Barney and Beanie Babies, but what kind of problem might those lunch boxes pose for him out in the world? A girl may wonder if she can give in to the impulse to buy a ballerina lunch box, or if that would make her cohorts think she aspires to *be* a ballerina, and then they might make fun of her, especially if she wasn't already enrolled in lessons and couldn't demonstrate right there in the lunchroom that she knows how to do a pirouette.

I once stood for thirty-five minutes in the lunch-box section of Kmart, periodically saying, "Okay, now, this isn't the most important decision you'll have to make in your life. Just pick *something*, and let's get over to the pants and shirts section." This was wrong of me. I should have shut up and read a book.

"But what if nobody likes Ninja Turtles anymore?" my son wanted to know.

"What would be the problem?" I said. "You like them. That's all that matters."

He looked at me as if I were crazy. "I'd have to carry Ninja Turtles all year," he pointed out. "It could get bad."

After what seemed like hours later, we settled for a Mickey Mouse lunch box—bright blue, with Mickey drawn in a tasteful black, of course, and looking very pleased with himself. He might have been dancing. At any rate, it was a classic look—restrained, unassuming, in the mainstream without crying out for approval; whimsical, without being too frothy.

"I think you made a wise choice," I said.

"You never know," he said grimly, "but at least I think this will be safe."

Hard as picking out the lunch box is, it's worse if you have a kid who doesn't think about this before school starts—as, quite honestly, some kindergartners don't. Some of them think it's still going to be all right to operate as though their nursery school friends are going to be leading the pack, instead of real grown-up elementary school kids. My friend Bonnie had a child who rashly picked a Tinky Winky lunch box without giving the matter much thought—and after her first week of school, she announced she had to drop out.

"What is it, darling?" said Bonnie, who had prided herself on the Kindergarten Preparedness books she'd been reading all summer long and knew that her daughter was A-1 kindergarten material. "Don't you like your teacher?"

"Yes."

"And you seem to like doing your work there. You're doing really well."

"It's not that."

"Is it the other children?"

"I just don't want to go there anymore. Call the school and tell them I'm staying home."

You guessed it—it was the Tinky Winky problem. Bonnie didn't figure it out, but my child delicately explained to me that anyone over the age of three cannot be associated with any Teletubby whatsoever and expect to have friends on the playground. The occasional, strong-willed child *might* be able to pull off such a thing by pretending to be affected by a case of fun-loving nostalgia—"Remember when we were babies and liked *Tinky Winky?*"—but for the average, just-starting-out kindergartner, it was too heavy a social burden to have to bear.

There were only two possibilities: lose the Tinky Winky or take up smoking unfiltered cigarettes on the playground.

Bonnie's daughter chose the first. One day on the school bus she simply hurled her lunch box out of an open window onto a street far from her house.

"I lost it," she told her mother later. "Tinky Winky just ran away."

"We'll get a new one," said Bonnie. "Maybe the store has more Tinky Winkys."

Her daughter frowned. "Mom, could I buy my lunch at school this year instead?"

The first day

Here's what you must pack for the first day of school: the lunch box, a pencil, a backpack to carry them in, and an entire box of tissues. Most of these items will go to school with your child. The tissues, of course, are for you, at the bus stop, one of the saddest places on earth.

Almost no one can survive the first day of school at the bus stop. I once saw two grown men in suits fall to their knees, clutching the shrubbery and bellowing with sobs, the minute the school bus had pulled away from the curb. They had held together pretty well until some unruly third-grader had let it slip that the bus driver's name was Killer, right before the bus careened up to the curb and all the little children trooped on.

Their kids—two five-year-olds who carried Baby Bop lunch boxes and wore twirly skirts with T-shirts with puffy animals sewed on—sweetly turned at the top step of the bus to wave good-bye. One, a darling in blond sausage curls, stuck her thumb in her mouth to give a few frantic sucks before she bounded inside to find a seat near Killer.

Naturally the fathers sobbed. There wasn't a dry eye anywhere near that stop sign.

So all the moms and dads stood around for nearly an hour, passing out tissues, the experienced parents trying to buck up the inexperienced ones, insisting that it would all be okay. We even explained that Killer had been driving the bus for years, that he had done nothing to earn that nickname (at least not in the recent past), and we even managed to remember some good deeds Killer had done, like braking at many railroad crossings. At last we all dried our tears and agreed to get on with the day, if we could. One fellow said he thought he might just ride over to the school just to make sure everything was going fine, to see—ha-ha—if Killer had managed to get the bus actually *there*.

"Don't," I could have told him. But it was no use. He was determined to see the school for himself, to see his little child clamber down the bus steps and find her way to her classroom.

I, too, was one of those who rode along to the school building, following the school bus while tears streamed down my cheeks. On my way, the radio played "Take Good Care of My Baby." I ran into the building, found the kindergarten room, with its bright colored paper flowers taped to the windows, its rows of blocks and preprimers, its lined paper, its blackboards, its pretty, smiling teacher standing at the front of the class in a pink dress. I burst in with another mother, and we stood at the back of the room, our chests heaving with the effort of not sobbing while watching our tiny children be indoctrinated.

Finally, once the class was having its milk-and-cookies break, the teacher made her way over to us. She was the same one I remembered from the Kindergarten Readiness Test.

"Remember my little boy?" I said, talking fast. "He's the one who had to turn his brain on. I hope you'll realize that he really can't stand it if anybody yells at him. If he does something bad, could you just look at him without smiling and not say anything? Maybe you could yell at the kid next to him instead. He's really quite sensitive and he would never knowingly hurt anybody—"

My friend piped up. "And my daughter is very scared about coming to kindergarten and really worried that you might think she's not smart enough—"

We all looked over at her daughter, who was cheerfully pounding her cookies into dust while her peers looked on in admiration.

"Listen," said the teacher in a voice just above a whisper. "You might as well go home and enjoy the peace and quiet. By the time you get there, it'll be time to come back anyway—and I don't think you want to live out the entire kindergarten year standing right here. Besides," she said, winking, "we don't beat them and scream at them the first day anyway."

We both laughed a little nervously.

Then we went to a coffee shop together, cried over the whole thing, and went back to the school to pick up our kids. Our thirteen minutes were just about up.

Cool stuff, like milk squirted out of the nose

You might be shocked when you sit down at the dinner table in the next few weeks, and realize that you're dining with a whole new person. You are suddenly living with a person who knows how to perform a loud, three-octave belch on demand, who can recite "Teacher, teacher, I declare, I see someone's underwear" up to one hundred times in a row without taking a breath, and best of all, can squirt a steady stream of milk from both nostrils.

If you were five years old yourself, you would be in awe of this person. As it is, your main reaction might be to take your own dinner into the kitchen to eat it while staring out the window and weeping quietly.

"Two weeks of kindergarten!" you screech to your spouse once the two of you have mopped up the milk, persuaded your child that belches and bawdy songs have no place at the dinner table, and have even finally wrestled your little angel into bed. "If it's like this after two weeks, what's it going to be like for the next twelve years of school?"

I say it's important not to contemplate the vastness of time at a moment like this, if you can possibly help it. You have to be like those people with "One Day at a Time" bumper stickers on their cars, from Alcoholics Anonymous. Only you are taking it one belch at a time, says my friend Laura. Concentrate on cleaning up the right nostril's milk spill, and then the left one's. Try not to think about a whole hideous future of nostril milk. It only serves to make the heart sore.

No one knows for sure why kindergarten does this to kids. Maybe it's because at last they feel themselves to be part of a larger system, where they are one of many inmates all romping through the asylum. They see quickly that they wildly outnumber the adults in charge—and that even though that may have been technically true at nursery school as well, at nursery school they never saw such a vast swarm of children collected together. Now they perceive their power. Now they know that they really do hold the future in their hands, and that there's something subversive about chanting that they've seen someone's underwear. Just a few short months before, you had trouble getting them to agree even to *wear* underwear when they would so much rather go naked—and now underwear itself has taken on the thrill of the forbidden.

You go in at night after they're asleep, wondering how somebody who looks just the same as before, with those plump baby cheeks and fat round little hands, can already be changing so much on the inside. All from just a few weeks of kindergarten. Who could imagine?

The princess in the office

My daughter hadn't been in kindergarten for two full weeks when she came home ready to cry.

"I'm not going back. Things are terrible there," she said, "and I think they're going to throw me out."

"Why would they throw you out?" I said. "You're great."

"*You* might think I'm great," she said, "but there they think I'm little."

It turned out that being little was a major sin in kindergarten. If you were unruly or hyperactive, the teacher didn't call you a juvenile delinquent and a pest, as she was thinking. Instead she said, "Are you too *little* to be here?"

One day—the Day of Reckoning—the teacher sat the whole class down on the round rug in front of the blackboard and said that some kids seemed as though they might be too little to stay in the kindergarten class, and they might be moving them somewhere else. They might go back to nursery school or, worse, back home with their mothers.

She looked around the room very sorrowfully. "I don't want this to happen," she said, "but if you're too little to be here, then that's probably the best thing—to wait and come back when you're bigger."

My daughter had been stunned by this news. "I learned to count to one hundred and twenty—but what can I do about how big I am?" she asked me. She threw herself at my shoulder, sobbing. "Everybody can see I'm the littlest one in the room!"

I explained that the teacher meant something else by little, not what size you were. She looked uncertain—and sure enough, the next day she was back again, with more bad news.

"Did you know they have a princess in the school, and if you're bad, you have to go see her?"

"There's not a princess, sweetheart—"

"Oh, there is! And she doesn't like it when kids run in the halls or if they talk in the lunchroom, or they fight on the playground. Then you have to go see the princess and she yells at you. She's a yelling princess."

"That's the principal," I said. "She's not a princess. She's the head of the school, and she's there to make sure kids follow the rules at school."

"Maybe," she said, "when *you* went to school they had a principal. But now today the schools get their own princess—a mean one. She's so mean she gets her own office, and nobody ever wants to go see her." She lowered her voice. "I think she might even eat some little kids."

Kindergarten really doesn't change much. When I was a kid, we had a principal who was suspected by the children of having eaten a little boy who was bad. She was a heavy woman with piles of white hair and a square jaw, and when she came to visit classrooms, kids tried to hide under the desks. We quaked when she spoke to us and refused to meet her eyes. Once I forgot my lunch from home, and when she heard about it, she said I should come into her office and share hers. She was smiling with big, white teeth.

I said no thank you. I was sure she'd serve me an arm or leg of that missing little boy, all spread out on a piece of bread. In fact, I remember sitting perfectly stiffly in her office, hoping she didn't bring out the Child Grinder to use on me. I was ready to run at the first sign of trouble.

My best friend Debbie breathed a sigh of relief when I was released, alive, back in the classroom. She had lots of questions for me: "Did she seem like she was going to bite you? Did you see any parts of bodies? What are her teeth like? Did the school secretary look worried?"

I think it would have earned me lots of points if I could have reported she was a princess. Too bad I didn't know that back then.

Living with an official member of the system

Soon after your introduction to the three-octave belch and the bawdy songs from the playground, you will have another huge realization. You will discover that you are living with a very Official Person, a member of the system. They have taken your child and are molding her into a Citizen.

You didn't expect this. Nor did you expect her to realize that you, try though you do, are actually running a slouchy kind of household. Oh, sure, you may be able to manage the three-meals-a-day thing, and get most of your family members bathed every day—but you are definitely lacking in the kind of organizational skills that kindergartners regard as critical to good life management.

Like notices, for instance.

You will not believe how many notices kindergartners bring home, and how vital it is that these notices be kept track of, every minute of every day. You probably think it's okay to haul them out of the backpack, put them on the kitchen counter or hang them on the refrigerator magnets, and consult them on an as-needed basis. There are some notices you might even think you can throw away.

No. The answer is no.

In your official capacity as the Parent of a Kindergartner, your chief job in the world is to unpack the notices, *commit them to memory*, then keep track of them until the end of time.

Your child will watch to make sure you do this, and give you periodic pop quizzes just to see that you're measuring up.

"Did you read that notice I brought home last Thursday?" he'll ask, usually when you're on the telephone. "Did you do what it said to do?"

"It didn't say to do anything," you'll explain. "I read it and threw it away."

"You *threw away a notice?*" His eyes go wild. The pupils bulge out.

It is no good to explain that people are allowed to throw away notices once they've been read. One day I threw out a notice but forgot that it said to send snack money every day, and then I had to get a *second* notice that began, "Some parents didn't seem to realize . . ."

I lived under a cloud of suspicion for the rest of the school year. And it's possible that I'm still regarded as untrustworthy with pieces of paper, even years later.

Worse was the day I forgot to look in the backpack at all. My daughter discovered this fact one Saturday morning when she came into my room to see if I could recite the Friday notices from memory.

"I haven't gotten around to them yet," I explained pathetically, from the depths of fourth-stage sleep. She got up on the bed, looming over me.

"You've got to read the notices," she said, "or I could get in big trouble."

"But there's no school today. We can read them after the sun comes up."

"You were *supposed* to read them right when I came home. You're *supposed* to get them out of my backpack right away and read them right then. The teacher said we have to make our parents read the notices *right when we come home.*"

So we held an Official Reading of the Notices at 6:22, and then everyone went back to sleep. At noon, I somehow passed the quiz on what the notices had said. I knew that if it was a snow day, you were supposed to listen to the radio. I remembered there was going to be a guest speaker at the PTA meeting in October.

Life settled down a little.

But a few days later, she said to me, "So do you ever say the President's Agents?"

"Excuse me?" I said.

"The President's Agents for the witches' dance. It's very important to say every day."

"I—I don't really know what you mean."

"Everyone who lives in our country should say it every day. You mean you *never* say it?"

"The President's Agents?"

"Yes. I will say it for you. 'I president's agents to the flag of the Newnited Stapes of America. And to the mapublic for witches' dance, one nation, under God, with Justin and riverty for all.'"

"Oh," I said. "That's the Pledge of Allegiance. Well, I used to say it in school, but now I really don't find so many opportunities."

"Well, I'm already saying it at school for myself, but I could say it with you on home days. You might need to get Daddy to help you on the other days. Maybe you could say it at night before you go to sleep."

I started to explain that, really, this is one of those things that hardly ever comes up in regular life after, say, twelfth grade—but I knew it wouldn't do much good. I could see that light in her eyes, that she was a convert to the system. I was already found derelict in my duties, after the snack money fiasco. I'd do well to keep my head down and say the President's Agents with her on the weekends—but maybe for the daily one I could get away with a simple promise to do the witches' dance.

Givesies, Backsies, and the Law of Jinx

The Official Rules of the School System, however, are nothing, *nothing*, compared to the stuff that goes on during playtime. That's where the really terrifying regulations get enforced.

On the playground, you see, they have the Law of Jinx.

My children have explained this to me. When you're operating under the Jinx constitution—and who in kindergarten can escape this?—then you get to yell "Jinx!" at the top of your lungs if you and somebody else happen to say something at the same time. (I presume this doesn't refer to the President's Agents, which, of course, everybody has to say in unison.)

"How does this help you, yelling 'Jinx' at somebody like that?" I wanted to know.

"Help you?" I got that incredulous look again, the one I'm always getting from my kids. "It doesn't *help* you. If you yell 'Jinx' first, then that person can't talk anymore until somebody says their name."

It's a power thing. Naturally that person's friends, though, are going to pitch in really quickly and say the name—and then you have to wait for another simultaneous speech occurrence. Kindergartners, apparently, are prowling the jungle gyms, hoping for the coincidence of saying something at the same time as someone else. But sometimes, I was told, you might have to wait all day long for such a thing to happen.

Because of the rarity of a jinxing really sticking indefinitely, new Jinx stipulations have had to come about. If you're worried, for instance, about somebody coming along and breaking the Jinx you've cast, there's kind of an insurance clause you can invoke. Instead of just yelling, "Jinx!" you can yell, "Telephone Jinx!" This means that only *you* can say the name and release the spell. It's a little like the thrill of holding the only key to a jail cell, apparently. Nobody would break the Law of Jinx; it would be social suicide.

And people think it's easy to be a little kid.

Allie, my middle daughter, explained that one day two

kids yelled "Telephone Jinx!" at the same time, and the whole playground came to a halt. Fourth-graders—almighty fourth-graders—had to be brought in to deliberate on what should happen next. This is a little like having a Supreme Court justice come down to small claims court, I gathered. Legally, of course, both people yelling "Telephone Jinx!" at the same time meant that neither party could ever speak again, and would probably have to live out the rest of their lives in religious orders.

However, some fourth-grader with the wisdom of Solomon decided that, after one hour had passed, the two people could face each other, silently (of course) count to three together by waving their fingers in the air, and then speak each other's names at the same precise second. Any imprecision on anyone's part—someone leaping ahead and shouting the other's name before counting to three—well, that would result in the Telephone Jinx being in effect until twenty-four hours had passed, when they would be allowed to try again.

"Wow!" I said when I heard this. "These are tough rules."

"You've got to be very, very careful on the playground," said Allie.

Not only is there Jinx to contend with, but also Givesies and Backsies. These, it seems, are garbage disposal systems. Let's say you have a candy wrapper you want to get away from. You hand it to someone else while yelling "No Backsies!" Then that person has to find someone else to stick it with. But there's a catch. The third person, having observed that there's a candy wrapper going around, can in advance say, "No Givesies," and then refuse to accept it.

If you're really mean, my daughter said, you can say, "No Givesies, no Backsies," when you palm off your trash, but that's frowned upon by polite society because it ends the game. More exhilarating is when the trash circulates along an entire lunch table, with everybody shouting, "No Backsies!"

"That's when you know you have some fun going on," Allie said.

And don't forget Twisties and Crossies. Crossies, of course, is when you don't have to tell the truth because you've got your fingers crossed behind your back. But Twisties—now, there's a stroke of genius from the new generation.

"When you call Twisties, it means you don't have to tell the truth because your hairs are crossing each other," said Allie.

It's a cruel and colorful world out there when you're five years old. And even more so sometimes when you simply live with a five-year-old. You'll be startled to hear yourself getting into the program.

One day you'll just naturally say something like, "Please take out the trash, no Givesies, no Backsies—and did you clean up your room? No Twisties, no Crossies."

And hey, every now and then, you'll get in a victorious "Telephone Jinx!"

And then your child has to be quiet until *you* get tired of the silence.

Show-and-tell

One of the things you probably didn't realize when you became a parent was that you were going to need objects that could be taken to school for show-and-tell. Lots of objects.

Let me just tell you now—there are people who, by March of the school year, have broken under the pressure of this. It is not easy to come up with five things per week which can be hauled off to school and, worse, placed under the judgmental scrutiny of a class full of kindergartners. You may think you have a house filled with inconsequential items that could impress a bunch of five-year-olds, but you'll be surprised how soon the day comes that you realize everything in your household has been shown and told—short of your major appliances, of course, which you have repeatedly refused to rent a truck for.

Over the course of the kindergarten year, we sent in every one of our prized and even some of our not-so-prized possessions. Every toy, book, stuffed animal went to school, as well as most of the Christmas tree ornaments, photographs from our family album, and probably several things I don't know about and would be humiliated by if I did. (My friend Darlene suspects that her black lace bra might have been featured in the kindergarten lineup.)

One March morning I found myself running around gathering up the backpack, the permission slip for the field trip to the fire station, the pencils, folder, library book to be returned, jacket, hat, mittens—when I heard a loud wail from my child: "Oh, no! I don't have anything for show-and-tell!"

We had hit the wall.

"Skip it today," I said in a reasonable voice. "Just watch the other children instead."

"I can't!" she screamed. "Show-and-tell is my very favorite thing in the whole world! I have to take something!"

I scanned the room in panic, looking for something that would be interesting. The wall calendar with our schedules written on it? The emergency phone list by the phone? Some brown bananas in the fruit bowl? Perhaps these could demonstrate the life cycle of fruit.

"How about the tablecloth that Aunt Virginia gave us?" I said.

She laughed a little hysterically.

I rummaged through the junk drawer, listening for the sound of the school bus. "How about the dog's heartworm medicine? Or—I know!—the cleaning instructions from the humidifier! You could use them to point out how crazy life is that people don't even have time to read these kinds of things. I'm sure the kids would relate."

Then I hit what I was sure was the show-and-tell jackpot: a brochure sent to us by the company that sent us our spring bulbs. "You could pass this around and say this is what our garden might look like someday," I said. "This is perfect!"

She looked at me levelly. "Do you think kindergartners *care* what we *hope* our garden will look like?"

"Well, then, why don't you take one of the loose tiles from the bathroom floor and show them what happens when your shower leaks for four months straight? Or take the sponge the dog ate most of, to show what canine teeth prints look like."

Finally she decided on a doll she'd taken before, but which had a new outfit. This was a huge social risk and broke the first and most important rule of show-and-tell: you can't bring anything you ever brought before.

"I'll have to say I'm not bringing the doll, I'm really showing her clothes," said my daughter. "Brittany Spellman won't believe me, she'll say it's the doll, but that's not true. I can get everybody else to be on my side, I think."

She had told me the sad story of one boy who brought in the same show-and-tell item every day for months, and because of that he got so low on the social scale that he couldn't even get his friends to admire the way he could blow milk through his nose.

"It's too bad," said my daughter, "because he can blow milk out of his nose farther than anybody else." She shook her head. "I just don't understand why he didn't *see* that you can't bring the same thing every day. Why didn't he notice that?"

"What was the thing he brought?" I asked.

"He brought in his family's waffle iron."

"What?" (You will not believe how many times you are screeching *"What?"* to your kindergarten child.)

"It's a nice one—but kind of little," she said thoughtfully. "I'm tired of seeing it."

There are other, unwritten rules to show-and-tell also:

- You can't bring in any fast-food toys. Every kid has a million of those at home, and nobody—*nobody*—thinks there is anything special about them. If that's all you have to offer, then it's clear you have a pretty pathetic life and should have had the sense to keep quiet about it.
- You have to let everybody at least touch the thing you bring in. But it's smart to keep your eyes on it the whole time it's being passed around, because sometimes kids will say it got lost while it was going around the classroom.
- The teacher wants you to say where you got the object from, but it's uncool to give too many details. Most kids just say they don't remember.
- Never, never bring in any sleep toy, or anything that might be thought to be a sleep toy, no matter how cool or cuddly you think it is. There are some things that simply can't be lived down.

This time, love is forever

Kindergarten love is nothing like those babyish nursery school crushes. Back in day care and nursery school, if a girl wanted to get married, all she had to do was put on a veil in the housekeeping corner and eventually a bachelor might finish playing with his trucks and come over to marry her. Those who didn't want to be married would still come over for a visit, but they said they'd be her dog or cat, instead of a husband.

One day my friend Marcy told me she was mystified as

to why every day when she picked her daughter up from
nursery school, all the boys barked and meowed at her as
she got her jacket.

"Oh, they're her suitors who are too scared to get married," I explained. "The future commitment phobes."

She gave me a blank look.

"No, really. When a nursery school guy likes you but isn't
ready to make a real commitment, he decides to be your
house pet instead. Apparently that's less of a threat."

"Oh," she said. "Like college."

In kindergarten, the romance in the air is real and pal-
pable. And exhausting. When people have crushes on each
other in kindergarten, that's like the real thing. This could
lead to an actual relationship, and not just the house pet
variety.

My son came home from kindergarten one day and said
he was so tired he might have to go take a nap. Since this
was the first time in his life before or since that he'd actually
admitted the need for sleep, I was understandably a little
bit curious.

"I have two girlfriends," he said with a sigh. "And it's
getting very hard for me at school."

"What's the hardest part for you?" I asked him.

"It's tough to save two seats in the lunchroom," he said.
"I get one seat saved, and Katie sits down there, but then
Jennifer comes over and starts crying because David has sat
in the only other empty seat, and then she yells at David to
leave, and he gets mad and throws a cookie at her. Then
the lunch lady comes over, and she makes Jennifer go sit at
a table with the teachers' aides—and the whole time Jennifer is crying and then she says she's mad at me because I
didn't save her a seat. But Katie and David got there first."

You hate to see your child so beleaguered and world-
weary at five, as though they've guessed the essential truth
that life can be tough. "Why don't you pick which one you

like the most and just settle down?" I said. "Let another boy have a girlfriend."

He gave me a little smile. "Actually," he said, "I'm still deciding. That's why I want to go rest in my bed. I have to turn my brain on."

14

Your Life, Now So Interrupted It's Not Even Recognizable

You might be scaring single people

One day you will be somewhere out in public with your child, having what you imagine is a pretty rational discussion about something. Perhaps you are in the grocery store, calmly explaining that you won't buy drinking straws anymore since she shoved one in the dog's nose, or very gently mentioning to your son that he will get no more big-boy underpants until he promises to stop peeing in the houseplants. Your kid is shrieking at you that the dog *wanted* the drinking straw in his nose, and besides that, sometimes people *have* to pee in the plants. It *waters* the plants, and you should be happy he's helping out. Meanwhile, you are piling box after box of Rugrats macaroni and cheese into your cart, along with toddler diarrhea medicine, a rectal thermometer, and Flintstones vitamins—and amicably saying over and over again, "You never need to pee in the houseplants. Always pee goes in the potty"—and then you see, for the first time, *that look* on someone else's face.

It's unmistakable—the look of somebody who's scared to death. This is a person who, after this, is going to be doubling up on birth control for the rest of her life, if not abstaining altogether from contact with men. As she rushes past, you wonder if she's headed out to join a religious organization that prohibits speech altogether. It's likely she'll mention your family situation when the leaders ask her what motivated her to give up the rest of her life to God.

You'd like to stop her on the way out and explain that parenthood isn't as bad as it looks. "You get *used* to it," you'd say. "It's actually fun! You learn so much about yourself. And all the things that you thought would be just horrendous— the diapers, for instance—they're *nothing*. Believe me—just the delight of looking at this little person you *made*—it just fills you up with wonder every single day. Trust me: you'll love it!"

But you don't. And the reason is that suddenly you re- member watching a parent yourself, back a long time ago, when you were cool. I remember going to visit a friend after college, Debbie, who'd married and had a baby right away. By the time I got around to seeing her five years later, she had three little kids, had cut her hair Frank Sinatra style, and had perfected a tone of voice that could freeze your brain cells before they could even form thoughts. I remem- ber leaping in the air in terror when she suddenly, midcon- versation, screamed, "All right, busters! *Who put the green Jell-O in the dog's ears? I want you to scrape it out immediately!*" Then she turned back to our conversation and said brightly, "So have you and your boyfriend talked any more about marriage and kids? Because it's really great—there's noth- ing like it, you know!"

If you've had any kind of decent upbringing at all, you don't want to take someone like that aside and point out how hideous everything about their lives is. Who knows how thin the web of self-delusion is that's holding her together? I fought back the impulse to laugh hysterically, but when I was about to leave, she said sweetly, "Just remember that when you're ready, parenthood is the most rewarding thing in the whole world. You'll just love it. It gets better and better every single day—*Jonathan, I said not to walk on top of the stove, and I meant it!*—We're just so much closer now that we have kids together. *If you break your neck, I'm not coming to the funeral, young man, believe me! Now get* down *before I come kill you myself!*"

Frankly, I've always been appreciative of Debbie's willingness to be the Parenthood Guinea Pig for our entire high school crowd, although all the rest of us were mystified as to how she could keep claiming she had anything resembling a bearable life. We figured that was what she had to say in order to ensnare others into parenthood. Maybe, we thought, they pay you off at the hospital if you promise not to spread the word about how bad life can get. Maybe you even get a bonus if you insist with all your might that you wouldn't trade this experience for anything and that it's enhanced your relationship with your husband. What a laugh!

Actually, though, now that I've had three kids, I think it may be something of a public service to scare people about parenthood. I mean, if they can't cope with a few temper tantrums in the supermarket and pee in the houseplants, then maybe they are better off drinking their margaritas with all the other single people and leaving the rest of us alone. I have a friend who decided never to have children after merely one trip to the beach with our family. True, she did have to ride home from the beach in our backseat, squashed in between the baby and toddler car seats—and true, she did get thrown up on once and got a lollipop stuck in her hair (rolled up into her hair, actually; it required a hack saw to remove it), and she was forced to answer the question, "Why?" almost six dozen times during the forty-minute ride. Later, though, she claimed that in addition to those indignities, one of our kids smeared purple sunscreen lotion all over her white silk blouse, the baby ate her sterling silver earring, and that she'd gotten diarrhea from the hot dog our toddler force-fed her in the car. (I didn't want to remind her that we hadn't eaten hot dogs at the beach, and that that particular hot dog had been located under his car seat cushion and probably predated his sister's birth six months earlier.)

I apologized, of course, but deep down I was thinking she was just the tiniest bit whiny. Doesn't everyone know not to take a white silk blouse to the beach, and not to eat a petrified hot dog with green fur on it?

Frankly, I can understand my friend Linda's approach. She was once riding on an airplane trip to Florida with her twin toddlers who wanted to rampage up and down the aisle, smearing apple butter, Velveeta-cheese-and-cracker paste all over the other passengers. It was horrible, she said, putting up with all the dirty looks she was getting from all the well-dressed single people on their way to an exotic vacation. Finally, after a third attempt to wrangle the twins into their seat belts while they shrieked, she stood up and said to the people around her: "You think being a parent is easy? Take a look! This is what daily life is—and it's not even the worst day we've had so far! So if you're scared of this, then do yourself and the world a favor and don't have any kids!"

That's when her son threw up Velveeta cheese and apple butter all over her wool suit. Some passengers lunged for their own air sickness bags.

"Still not the worst day we've had!" she called out.

Measuring up to Timmy's mom

I don't know how to break this to you gently, but Timmy's mom is doing a much better job of things than you are. Timmy's mom lets Timmy have a television set in his room, and he can watch it anytime he wants to, even late at night. Timmy has a pool and a puppy, and he doesn't have to take a bath every night because he just goes into the pool with the puppy and they play for hours. Also, he has every Nintendo game ever made, and he sleeps in pajamas that were made for the captain in *Star Trek*, who happens not to need them anymore so he gave them to Timmy. And Timmy gets to bring Burger King food to school for lunch, and his mother doesn't even mind that he's drinking Coke instead of the pukey milk everybody else has to drink. And oh, by the way, Timmy can *drive*. His mother lets him drive the car when they go to the store.

"She does not," you say. Here you were, buying the bit about the pool, the puppy, the baths, even the Coke at school, but now the *Star Trek* pajamas and the driving have shown you what you're dealing with. Timmy's obviously a pathological liar.

"She does! She does! Timmy told me that he drives to the store all the time."

"Well, Timmy isn't telling you the truth."

"Timmy always tells the truth! He drives, and he gets to steer right into the parking lot. Once a policeman saw him, and the policeman just waved. Because the police all know there's a boy who can drive because his mother lets him."

It will hardly help to tell you not to even get into this argument with your own child, because of course you have to. You can't help it. Even if you wanted to coolly say, "That's nice, dear, very nice for Timmy indeed—but no, you can't skip baths, get a pool, a puppy, every Nintendo game, and have a television set in your room. So sorry," and have it be done with, you can't.

Instead, you stand there, ticking off for him why none of this could be true. You explain that the captain of *Star Trek* doesn't even *know* Timmy, much less share his cast-off clothing with him. And that no police officer is ever going to let a little kid drive, whether his mother thinks it's a good idea or not. You even go into the evils of Nintendo, television in kids' rooms, and nonbathing—and all of it is to no avail. Your child sits there with a frowny face while you bat your logic and commonsense words at him.

Timmy's mom is doing a better job than you. And that's all there is to it.

Okay, so you're going to have to meet this Timmy's mom. At the next cupcake-making event for the school, or the very next field trip that requires mothers to be in attendance, you'll go and look her over. You half expect to see her wearing some of the *Star Trek* captain's cast-off suits and to drive up on a Harley. No doubt she's at least carrying a portable Nintendo in her purse.

But no. She is, you're a little disappointed to see, just an ordinary woman. She has the same hunted, frazzled look that everybody else has. Not only that, but her cupcakes are lopsided and half of the frosting has slid off. She has to run off early because her youngest child has bitten somebody at nursery school, and the administrators are insisting she come and collect him. He will probably need psychiatric evaluations and possibly special schools, you think.

As she heads back to the parking lot, you want to stop her for a moment and just clear up a couple of things—the *Star Trek* pajamas and the driving, perhaps—but it's clear she's in a hurry. She smiles at you and for a moment you see in her eyes the same bewildered look you see in your own. She's on your wavelength. And you smile back.

And as you look over at your own child, whispering something to his classmate, for the first time you wonder what delightful spells he's weaving about *his* home life. *My mom lets me stay up all night and I never have to brush my teeth, and I get a million dollars for allowance every week. No, no, don't ask my mom about it. She doesn't like to talk about all the cool stuff I do.*

The *fatigue*

Somebody started a rumor that it's only when you have a tiny baby—of the nonsleeping variety—that being a parent makes you tired. Otherwise, the whole thing is just a snap. It's a breeze. A walk in the park. In fact, it's *better* than a walk in the park, because you get to be looked up to. It's a walk in the park when you're the park ranger. After all, you're now the expert, somebody's idol, the person who gets to be the boss.

I don't know how these ugly rumors get started, or why so often it will seem that you're the only one who isn't getting anything that resembles actual rest. Forget eight hours of sleep a night; that's a pipe dream. But why can't you focus your eyes anymore or remember your social security number?

Frankly, when you're the parent of a preschooler, most of the time it feels as though somebody's come along and whacked you with a big board. You're in a daze, not remembering where your keys are, what you're supposed to fix for dinner, where you put that file at work that you carried around for a solid hour and then suddenly couldn't lay your hands on. You didn't show up for a hair-cutting appointment last week, your kid hasn't been to the dentist in over a year but you can't seem to remember to call during office hours, and you left the wet laundry in the washer all weekend, and now it's all mildewed.

It's no wonder that you now go to sleep every night at eight-thirty, during your attempts to get your child wrestled into submission. I have been known to fall asleep during the bedtime ritual every night. In fact, bedtime got to be known as "the time we put Mommy to sleep."

Each night I'd climb the stairs at eight o'clock, thinking

that as soon as the kids were asleep, I'd come right down and finish up the dinner dishes, pay some bills—or even, wonder of wonders, have some Quality Time alone with my husband. And each night, somewhere after the tooth-brushing ordeal and the reading-a-story ordeal, and the telling-a-story ordeal, but before (or during) the singing-three-lullabies ordeal, I'd conk right out. Sometimes the children would bounce back downstairs to have a little Quality Time alone with my husband. There I'd be, curled up in their soft little beds, smelling their sweet-smelling shampoo still on the pillow, way off in dreamland, while they were off living their regular evening lives.

There were times I woke up at midnight, to go downstairs and find all of them watching Letterman, or else the kids stretched out on the carpet like fallen warriors, with my husband asleep on the couch. Other times, they'd all come upstairs and dislodge me from my sleep, and I'd uncrook my neck, unkink my spine, and try to learn to walk upright again.

Once my friend Diana, who did not have the good sense to go out and get married and reproduce herself, asked me what I'd like for my birthday. At first all I could think of was an hour in the bathtub to myself.

She tried to be polite, but you could see she thought that was a pathetic thing to want. "Who would interrupt you in the bathtub, anyway?" she said. "Just unplug the phone, and you won't be interrupted."

Who would interrupt anybody in the *bathtub*? I couldn't believe anybody would ask such a question. The phone is the least of it. Who *wouldn't* need to get in there when somebody's taking a bath? What if your pet frog needs more water? What if you need a couple hundred Band-Aids to stick all over yourself? What if somebody eats a piece of cheese and it's bigger than the piece of cheese that you got? How are you going to measure something like that and see that justice is done, if you don't get into the bathroom where your mother is in the tub? Besides that, let a mother get in the tub, and at least two of her own kids and maybe even some neighborhood kids will need to come in and poop.

"I never heard of this kind of thing," said Diana. "Just lock the door and tell them to leave you alone."

"Oh, no, you don't want to lock the door when you're in the tub," I said. "Then all hell breaks loose. The noises, the screams, the threats. It's when they think they can't interrupt you that they get unbelievably dramatic."

But on second thought, I realized I didn't really care about an uninterrupted hour in the tub. I'd only worry the whole time anyway, especially if I hadn't thought to tie them up before I got in the tub. No, it would be far better—far more healthful, even—to have eight hours of sleep.

"No, no," I said. "Make it ten hours of sleep. I'd say twelve, but that sounds too greedy. And I might get a headache if I had that much sleep all at one time. It could be a shock to the system."

She was looking at me and shaking her head slowly. "Just look at yourself," she said. "All you want for your birthday is *sleep*. You don't want a night out with your husband—maybe a nice dinner in a good restaurant?"

"No," I said. "If I went to one of those places with the white tablecloths, all I'd be able to think about was bedsheets. I'd be out cold in two seconds."

"What about a weekend away with him?"

"Let everybody else go away. All I want is to sleep."

She studied me for a long time. Then she said, "Do you know I go to sleep whenever I'm bored, and there are weekends I sleep as much as fifteen hours at a time?"

"Didn't your mother ever tell you it's not nice to brag?" I asked her.

Opposite Day

When you are just about as tired as you've ever been in your life, a day will come where you will say to your child something innocuous like, "Okay, go wash your hands for dinner." You are thinking that soon dinner will be over and done with, and it'll be that much closer to bath time, story time and bedtime. You have only a few hours of hard labor to go before you get to close your own eyes. "Go wash your hands," you say, to celebrate this realization.

But instead of scampering off to wash her hands, your child will laugh uproariously. You have just said the funniest thing in the world.

"I'm glad you like this idea," you say. "Now, quick, go wash your hands so we can eat."

"So! You want me to slow down and get my hands as dirty as I can so we can throw up?"

Don't even try to figure out what's going on. I'll tell you. You've entered Opposite Day. This is a day when no means yes, and yes means no—and everything you say is totally backward.

It takes a lot of concentration to live through an Opposite Day. That's why children invented it. They want to test your concentration as much as possible. It's a service kids perform for the adult brain.

But you still have a few operating brain cells, so you say, "Go get your hands dirty for breakfast," and your child tells you, "I will get as dirty as possible"—and marches off to wash her hands. All is fine until after supper when you say, "Take your plate into the kitchen, please," and the child says, "Ohhh, so you've decided we're going to be slobs and leave our plates on the table all night?"

That's when you see that you are going to have to completely change your brain settings and remember to say the opposite of what you mean every single time. No more taking time off to think about where your house keys might be, and wondering if you're wrinkling too fast, or whether you should have taken Latin in high school. It's going to take a lot of brain wattage to remember to say yes every time you mean no and no every time you mean yes. You'll be lucky if you can remember *not* to use Opposite Day terminology on the people at work.

Sometimes Opposite Day just disappears on its own, a neat experiment that everybody gets tired of once the whole family has the hang of it. But I should warn you that some children really want to take it to its furthest reaches. That's how it came about that one time I found myself in a conversation with a kid about the opposite of ice cream.

"Do you think the opposite of ice cream is spinach?" he wanted to know.

"I don't think so," I said.

"Well, then, what *is* the opposite of ice cream?" he said.

"I don't think ice cream has an opposite. It's a thing, and things don't have opposites."

"Well, then, what's the opposite of a chair?"

"Nothing is the opposite of a chair."

"Ha! A table is the opposite of a chair!"

"Is it?" I said. This was beginning to remind me of a philosophy course I took freshman year in college, when we spent hours discussing whether the chairs stayed in the room when we couldn't see them. But I don't think we ever talked about whether tables were the chairs' opposites—or even whether the tables stayed in the room. I suppose they did whatever the chairs did.

"Another thing I want to know," he said. "If you tell me to take a bath, is the opposite of that to *not* take a bath, or is to roll in the mud?"

"I think the opposite would be not to take a bath."

"Hmmm," he said. "That's good. I don't like to roll in the mud."

"Wonderful," I said. "I can see we're going to get along just fine."

He laughed. I had fallen for Opposite Day one more time.

Your pals you never get to see

One thing nobody mentions much about parenthood is how much trouble you have to go to just to see your regular friends anymore. Something about creating a family causes you to use up most of your viable hours keeping the family going—and one day you look up and realize that instead of seeing your friends, you are busy seeing only pediatricians, baby-sitters, and nursery school personnel. If you're not careful, these people become the ones you're telling your troubles to: how you couldn't decide whether to highlight your hair or just chop the whole damn mess of it off, and how your sister is going to marry that creep after all, and what are family Thanksgivings going to be like from now on?

Don't make this mistake. Pediatricians are wonderful, caring people, but when you stop talking about the kid's booster shots and stray into your sister's love life, they give you a funny look and start to back out of the room. This is as it should be. They probably have their own problems to contend with, not the least of which is they have to see forty more patients before they can go home and see their own kids, and you certainly don't want to interfere with that. You probably can't get them to solve your sister's love life anyhow—and as a general rule, it's always better *not* to cut your hair completely off.

But you do need your friends. And you probably need them even more now that you have a child in your life. It's important to have someone you can tell the *real* stuff of your life to, who won't think you're an unfit mother because moths flew out of the oatmeal carton this morning—and you considered cooking the oatmeal and serving it to your child anyhow. (You *didn't* serve it, but it was a close call.) You need someone who can tell you that you really were so smart to buy all that toilet paper on sale, even though it does mean you have to keep it behind the couch in the living room, where all a guest has to do is peek over the back and see thirty-seven rolls of Charmin right there on display. You need someone that you can sob to when it's eleven-thirty at night, and you've cleaned up approximately 4,900 gallons of diarrhea and throw-up in one afternoon, which each time meant even washing the kid's *hair*, because of the projectile way it flew around the room (someday this will be the funny part of the story, your friend points out), and you were so scared when his temperature spiked up to 104, and how you sat for hours with him on your lap, and he was so hot it felt like he was burning a hole in your lap, and that once he fell asleep, you started to cry.

No, you need a friend—even if it's somebody you only see once a month at the playground or can talk to when it's nearly midnight. My best friend and I once conducted our friendship through shouts from the car windows as we waited in the car-pool line—and one time we were ecstatic to happen to meet at the meat counter of the grocery store. Oh, sure, other customers were furious with us because we were blocking the chicken thighs section in our frantic rush to catch up on each other's lives, but once they moved us aside, over by the beef livers, life went on as smoothly as before.

Whatever you have to do to see your friends, it's worth it. After all, you need somebody to remind you that this is just a temporary stage of life. And somebody who doesn't think you're a bad mother because for one tiny second you considered serving moth larvae. And somebody who can make you laugh, whether you served the moth larvae or not.

The minivan

The hardest thing about your new life as a mom might just be the minivan. Somewhere between the pregnancy test and the day the first kid goes to kindergarten, it seems to show up in the driveway—and for good, solid, practical reasons, of course. After all, if you're going to have to carry most of your household with you everywhere you go—and it seems that you are—then you might as well have a vehicle that can hold it all. You may have sworn you weren't going to sink so low as to purchase the symbol of all that turns exciting people into parental drudges, but like all the rest of us, the day comes when you realize that your little sports car that you had before you got married can't stand up to the wear and tear of children—and neither can the pickup truck you drove around in college, with your Labrador retriever and a cooler in the back.

The trouble is this: For some reason when you get into the minivan, it seems you're always on your way to Toys "Я" Us for the latest action figure fad toy, or else to the grocery store to buy another box of Lunchables or Rugrats macaroni and cheese. A minivan fairly screams, "Car pool!" It never screams, "Love tryst!"

Sometimes it screams, "Here comes someone who's become boring, now that she has kids!" I think minivans are preprogrammed to stop at all toy stores, elementary schools, and late-night pharmacies. They are definitely *not* programmed for taking you to the beach for a weekend of sleep, parties, and suntans.

When you're driving the minivan, you won't get waves from guys stopped next to you at red lights, or even people craning around to see what you look like. And even if you're heading for the gym to pump iron and work out, people seeing you in the minivan will automatically know you're going to the gym only because you're trying to lose that last ten pounds of pregnancy bulge so at least you won't have to continue wearing baggy jumpers or sweatpants for the rest of your life. They know. Oh, they know. They take one look at the minivan, and it tells them everything they need to know about you.

Minivans take on different kinds of trash collections, too. Whereas once your car trash consisted of cappuccino cups, CD cases, hair scrunchies, deposit slips from the bank, and manicure receipts, now your in-car garbage is likely to be something gooey and disgusting. Most likely it contains at least four wadded-up tissues containing something yucky that had to be spit out by a kid, as well as saliva-saturated things the kid tried to eat but found indigestible.

There are toys, pieces of toys, doll limbs and heads, ripped-up pages of books, former oranges, apple cores, half-empty and now crystallized juice boxes, banana peels mashed together with raisins that have turned rocklike, and many unidentifiable substances that it would take a scientific laboratory weeks to identify. Every now and then, you find you have to pull over to the side of the road and start checking underneath the seats just so you can find out why it smells as though something crawled in the car, drank fermented apple juice and a bunch of Swiss cheese, and then dropped dead. You are fully expecting to find a dead animal lurking there somewhere—but no, most likely it's just the regular smell of children and their possessions, confined to a minivan in all kinds of weather.

Believe me: a sports car may be great, but the ability to

drive down the road smelling a dead animal fermenting in apple juice—and still not gag—is a skill you'll have all your life.

Your telephone life

Before I had kids, I was telephone championship material. I want to be as modest as possible about this, but let's just say that if telephoning had been an Olympic sport, I really would have at least gotten a silver medal and possibly could have gone for the gold. That's how long I can talk on the phone to my friends before my ear gives out or I think of something I'd rather be doing. Like most women who grew up in the last half of the twentieth century, I learned to conduct my entire life—do housework, take baths, even get dressed—with a phone tucked under my chin.

But all that changed when I had kids. For one thing, children consider the phone a personal rival, and a challenge to their position as your offspring. You can explain all you want that you don't love the telephone in the same warm, satisfying way that you love your family, but kids will still be determined to shut down your conversations whenever and however possible.

They have lots of creative ways of doing this, too. The usual ones—crying, whining, falling down and getting hurt—work wonders, but to be on the safe side, they come up with even more innovative, phone-specific methods as well. My youngest figured out a way of wrapping herself in the phone cord while I'd talk. She would simply come and stand in front of me while I was talking, and then slowly start to rotate, and within seconds, she had the entire phone cord wrapped around her neck twenty times, and I was having to twirl in the opposite direction to untangle her and save her life. It does no good in a case like this to say, "Stop that right now, this instant!" or any of those commands that your mother used with you that worked so well. A child who seemingly is willing to die by strangulation in order to get you off the phone can't be dismissed simply with a reprimand.

For some reason that I have yet to figure out, whenever I was on the telephone, my kids seemed to need to have words spelled for them.

"How do you spell 'get'?"

"G. E. T."

"Now, how do you spell 'off'?"

"O. F. F."

"Now, how do you spell 'the'?"

"I'm on the phone! Can you please go play for a few minutes and then I'll come and talk to you and spell all the words you need?"

"Just one more word. How do you spell 'phone'?"

The other clever thing they do is pantomime. There you will be, hearing about your friend's California vacation and joining with her in speculation as to whether or not it's possible for single men to be *too* wealthy and *too* attentive, when you become aware that someone—possibly your child—is standing in front of you, mouthing something. You can't even tell if any sound is coming out.

You do what any person on the telephone would do: you turn in the opposite direction and continue with your conversation. "No," you are saying, "I never had a man say *that* to me." And then you see it again: a maddening little person in your field of vision, moving her mouth, eyes bugged out of her head.

So you mouth back in her direction: *"What?"* And listen to your friend, going on about the beach, the freeway system, the way men in L.A. look moments before they ask you out—and your child is now pantomiming something. Something dramatic, from the looks of it. Something *huge*.

"What?" you mouth again, and this time your friend says, "Did you *hear* me? The guy had a *gold Corvette!*"

"That's wonderful," you say. And mouth, "What?" to your child. Again.

"Wonderful?" she says. "How can you say it's wonderful when surely you remember how I feel about gold Corvettes ever since Howie ran off with Marlene—"

"Oh, right," you say. "Listen, something huge is going on here, and I've got to get off the phone and check it out. I'll try to call you once everybody has gone to sleep, but it might be sometime after midnight."

You get off the phone and look squarely at your child. "Now what is so important?"

"There's something amazing in the potty you should see," she says. "It could be *very* important."

You march off to the bathroom. "It had better be an entire fire-breathing dragon that's eating up the rest of the bathroom fixtures, the way you kept interrupting me. Now what is it?"

It is not a fire-breathing dragon. It is not even a spectacularly astonishing poop, which you have often been sent to admire. No. It's a routine floating piece of toilet paper that reminded your child of the smoke from a fire-breathing dragon's mouth.

"See? Doesn't that look like dragon smoke in the potty?" she says.

This is how brilliant children are. Deep down they know that nothing in the potty is going to be amazing enough to get a full-grown woman off the telephone—but simply through the art of pantomime, they can get her there every single time.

Whatever happened to the natural respect between parents and children?

I had a list of things that my mother always said that I was never going to utter in the presence of my children. Now I have said every one of them, sometimes every day.

- "Because I said so, that's why."
- "Get down off of there before you break open your head."
- "Someday you'll have children, and I hope you'll see how crazy you drove me!"
- "I'll give you something to cry about!"

I am not proud of the fact that I have said these things with such frequency, but sometimes they're the only phrases you can remember in a crisis. I'm not sure what the last one even means. I used to puzzle over it when I was a child, especially since it was always yelled when I was *already* crying—but like so much else that accompanies parenting, I know now that it doesn't have to mean anything specific; it's just to fill in the spaces while you try to figure out what else you can do to stop a situation from getting even worse.

Still, I had big plans to be Reasonable with my kids. We were going to have the kind of relationship where we would have Respect and Love for each other. They would obey me because of their great need to acknowledge respect for me, and to acknowledge my respect for them. Believe me, I could get tears in my eyes just explaining how this system was going to work.

When my kids were tiny, I joined a day-care cooperative with a bunch of like-minded people. And we went around respecting one another and ourselves and all the kids. Respect just oozed out of the place. No one ever said, "Because I said so, that's why!" It was truly wonderful there.

One day, in fact, I remember hearing a father respectfully trying to persuade his little three-year-old daughter to put on her coat so they could go home. But she didn't think that was a good idea, despite the fact that it was five-thirty and day care was closing and besides that, he was writing his doctoral dissertation and had about twenty minutes to get her home and fed and ready for bed, if he expected to finish his thesis by June.

So he patiently explained about the time and the need for the day care day to end, and his need to write his dissertation. After nearly every statement of his, she said, "Why?"

"Well, my love, it's five-thirty because that's the time it is when the sun has gotten to this point in the sky—"

"Why?"

"Because that's when day care has to close because it's going to be night."

"Why?"

"Because that's the way the world is. We have night and we have day."

"Why?"

"Because that's the way the universe was created."

"Why?"

"Well, that's not really something human beings totally agree on. Some think that—"

And on and on and on. When he got to the point where he was explaining the subject of his dissertation and the need to write it on time, and how *that* translated into the creation of the universe, and how that related to the need for her to put on her coat, I stepped over and touched him lightly on the shoulder.

"This is very admirable, what you're doing," I said. "Do you think you'll be done by morning?"

He said the way things were going, he very much

doubted it, that he was just waiting for me to leave so that he could finish things off the real way. "I just say, 'Melanie, get your coat—we're getting in the car!' And if she whines and asks why, I say, 'Because I said so, that's why. And if you don't stop, I'll give you something to cry about!' "

"Wow," I said. "Are you ever able to work in, 'Get down off of there before you break your head open'?"

"Usually once or twice while I'm cooking dinner," he said. "She likes to climb on the counters."

The moth hospital in a shoe box and the Glad-to-See-You fish in the bowl

Before you turn into a parent, when someone mentions the words "household pet," you're likely to think of a golden retriever, perhaps, or perhaps a nice tabby cat. Chances are, you don't think of toads from the yard—the kind you're going to be getting up every morning at five-thirty to catch flies for. Or the gypsy moth caterpillar who, after eating your maple tree, has now been given a home in a mustard jar in your kitchen.

But even if you have the more traditional, furry kind of pet at your house, your child is more likely to be drawn to those other kind.

You see, that's what is so great about little kids. One of the nicest things about them—when they're not bonking somebody over the head, that is—is their compassion. They may have issues with their human companions, but they are *always* willing to save the lives of the worms in the driveway and the moths that are eating the pasta products in your cupboard. Just let a kid get the idea that there is a tiny insect suffering somewhere, and she's right on the case, insisting that all life support options be used to bring it back to health.

That's why you will probably spend many hours with

the responsibility of bringing health and good cheer to a half-dead grasshopper at some time in your life. But let me warn you: most insects who have come in contact with a little child seem almost grateful to pass on to their Eternal Reward. You will detect a strong death wish about them, as you hold on to their limp little carcasses. You would like to put the thing out of its misery and go on with the business of living your life. But you can't. Your child is pleading, "Save Miranda's life, please! She's my best best friend in the whole world."

"You named this grasshopper?" you say. It seems to be a rule in the lives of children that anything with a name has to receive full-bore life support.

"She told me her name by herself," the child says. "But then she fell on the ground under my shoe, so we've got to save her. I'll get a Band-Aid."

We once operated an insect hospital in a shoe box for nearly a week. Our patients were the moth, Bradley, who in his larval stage, had most likely eaten my winter coat and couldn't fly anymore; a housefly named Craig who had only one wing; Miranda the squashed grasshopper; and Sarah, a cricket who had already passed away but hadn't been honored at a memorial service yet. The shoe box was filled with straw, bits of wool for Bradley (in case he should discover a bit of space for even one more molecule of food), a raisin, and a bowl of water—and we all had to take turns observing the decline of the creatures and trying to come up with solutions to better their lives. Neighborhood kids came by to sing the Barney theme song to the living, and I was so impressed that I agreed to let Sarah have a decent burial in the potted philodendron in the living room. I didn't know at the time that this would mean the roots to the plant would be mangled and that a gallon of potting soil would land on the carpet—but death and burial aren't always pretty, you know. You have to make sacrifices sometimes.

You will be doing well if your child does not end up blaming you for the death of her best friend, the tiny-animal-with-a-suicidal-streak. This is what goldfish do best: teach children something about the impermanence of life and the fact that *you* are most likely responsible for their deaths. That's why they cost so little at the pet store: the owners know that you have to come back and replace them once or twice a week to keep your child from being in a constant state of mourning.

Mostly when goldfish come to live at your house, they swim in dizzyingly slower and smaller circles, a look of boredom and doom on their odd little faces—and then one day you look into the bowl, and you discover they are swimming sideways or upside down, or some fool way. It's just a matter of time then until The End, when you need to go back to the pet store for a replacement fish. (I recommend keeping some replacement fish in a hidden aquarium in the closet, for those middle-of-the-night tragedies that fish are so prone to.)

But one time, through some fluke in the universe, we managed to keep a goldfish alive for months. This goldfish—named the Glad-to-See-You fish because of the way he swam to the side of the bowl to greet human beings as they came in the room—actually seemed interested in joining the family. My five-year-old was certain he listened to our conversations, held opinions on such topics as homework and television programs, and even missed us when we went away. One day, in fact, Ben decided he really shouldn't go to school because the fish missed him so much.

"He might die from being sad," he said.

"We can't suspend our lives because our goldfish needs someone to look at," I said, a little too hysterically. "And last time I looked, they didn't have day care for fish."

This conversation was taking place minutes before the school bus was to arrive, and yet it was clear that no one was going to be able to leave the house without at least one of us in tears. I'd already had a fight that morning with the two-year-old, who wanted me to pour out the soy sauce and put her apple juice in that bottle before she went to day care. And now I was being asked to suspend the rest of the day so that the goldfish wouldn't die of loneliness.

"I'll take him with me on the bus," said Ben.

"No. No, you won't. It is a known fact that goldfish do not get lonely, that they love the hours they have to themselves. You'll understand when you're older just how great a feeling that can be. Now we *have* to catch the school bus, so get your backpack, zip up your jacket, and let's go!"

I could see that he was about ready to cry, so I finally said, "Look. Why don't you tape a picture of yourself on the side of the fishbowl and then he'll have you to look at all day while you're gone?"

I was expecting the argument that the fish would know it wasn't the real Ben, but instead, he ran and got his school picture, we taped it on, and went about our lives.

Months later, though, I was responsible for a fish murder. We went to swim in a pond, and there Ben rescued a one-half-inch catfish and insisted we keep it alive in a paper cup for the rest of our lives. Naturally, after a few days, the paper cup started to disintegrate, so I carefully moved the fish into the measuring cup, where it swam around happily for a couple of days—until one morning when I was making oatmeal and realized I needed the measuring cup, preferably without a catfish in it.

That's when it hit me, that it should move into the fish bowl with the goldfish.

"No, no!" he screamed.

"It'll be fine," I said. I explained about how goldfish really only eat little flakes, not other fish, and catfish scoot along the bottom, sucking up algae. "It's a perfect match, you'll see," I said. "They'll be good friends."

But just as I carefully placed the tiny little catfish in the goldfish bowl, the Glad-to-See-You fish happened to be lazily swimming in his circle, and somehow—I swear this had to be accidental—the catfish just got sucked up into the Glad-to-See-You fish's mouth, where it stuck there. Ben screamed and fell to the floor. I stood there, stunned, not knowing what to do. And so naturally the phone rang.

"What?" I screamed into the phone. "Whoever this is, I've just accidentally fed a catfish to the goldfish, and now it's stuck in his throat, and both of them are going to die!"

It was my friend Chris. "Reach into the bowl, pick up the goldfish, and pull the catfish out of its mouth," he said calmly, as though this were something he'd done a million times himself.

"*Pick up the goldfish?* You mean, hold him in my hand?" Ben screeched from the floor.

"Yes. Just pick up the goldfish and remove the catfish."

"They'll both die!"

"And this way they'll both live? I don't think that goldfish is going to live long with a catfish sticking out of his mouth interfering with his eating mechanism."

So I did this. Predictably, the catfish was already done for. The goldfish was startled at being lifted, airborne, and having a fish removed from his mouth, but he went back to swimming in circles and staring at Ben's picture. I was castigated loudly for murdering fish; there was even some talk of calling the Animal Abuse Hot Line and reporting me. But in the end, it was ruled that I had simply made an ignorant mistake, not a willfully malicious one. (This was my ruling, actually.)

And after everybody got settled down, I had time to go off and reflect on the fact that, back when I was single and unencumbered, driving a Triumph Spitfire convertible and staying up all night listening to Led Zeppelin if I wanted, not once did I ever think I'd have to remove a catfish from a goldfish. Nor did I think I'd have the kind of goldfish who would require a photographic record of our presence so he could continue to live in a bowl.

I don't know why parenthood brings with it these little surprises—how it is that there are things you can only learn when you have a little kid in your life. I called Chris back later, to report that we still had one surviving fish. "How did you know to do that—to pick up the fish?" I asked.

"I knew you had to do something," he said. "With kids, it's important to look like you're trying, even if it's never going to work. So the goldfish really lived through that?"

"So far," I said. "We had the funeral for the catfish late this afternoon. He went into the philodendron plant, like the others."

Chris had to hang up. It was getting to be dusk, and the best mosquitoes are out then. He was personally responsible for keeping alive his kids' tree frog—a very particular eater, who would only accept the first, tender mosquitoes of dusk.

"Are we crazy?" I said.

"No. We're just parents," he said.

15

When I'm the Mommy and You're the Kid...

A day will come when your child is furious with you. Okay, the feeling is mutual—you can't quite believe she thought it would be okay to write with Magic Marker along the back of the white leather couch, especially after you'd explained a million times before that furniture isn't for writing on.

For her part, she's explaining that the couch looked like a giant white board, and she couldn't *help* writing on it. It was smooth and it was white and it was *clean*. . . .

Also, she says, she's mad that you're making asparagus for supper and that she heard you say you were going *out* with Daddy, and why would Daddy want to go out with you when *she's* planning to marry him just as soon as you leave? In fact, why don't you just go out by yourself, and she and Daddy can stay home all night and play games by themselves?

You try to get the subject back to the Magic Markers on the back of the couch, and how she just might have to go into her room and stay there for the rest of her life, when she says, consumed with fury, "When *I'm* the mommy, and you're the kid . . . you are really going to be sorry! You will have to stay in your room every day for your whole life!"

You stop talking. Not because you can't think of the next

thing to say, which obviously is, "You will *never* be the mother of me!" But because you remember, suddenly and clearly, saying that to your own mother. You remember standing in the kitchen in the old house, screaming at her and feeling so strongly that the day would come when she, the all-powerful mom, would be reduced to your powerlessness, and you would be the one standing there, wielding the punishment or being the one to say what was for dinner or when bedtime would be. And you remember how she laughed when you said that.

So the two of you work together on cleaning the markers off the couch. (Thank God Magic Markers are washable these days.) You talk about how this writing on the couch should never happen again. She says she's sorry. You don't send her to her room after that. Maybe you play Candy Land and let her win. You read her a story, pulling her close to you on the couch. You play your one-millionth game of Barbie and then help her rock the baby dolls to sleep. She pretends to nurse each one and then pats them as she pulls the covers up. Before she leaves the room, she sings them all a lullaby.

"You're a good mommy to your dolls," you say.

"Don't worry," she says, smiling. "I'll be a good mommy to you, too. When I'm the mommy and you're the kid, you can stay up all night if you want to. And you can always win the Candy Land games."

About the Author

SANDI KAHN SHELTON's work has appeared in *WorkingMother, Redbook, Woman's Day, Good Housekeeping, American Baby,* and *Salon.* She is the mother of three children and lives in Connecticut.